Pitman
Education
Library

Teaching in Further Education

Teaching in Further Education

G J Russell MA, Dip Ed

Head of Teacher Education Unit
Liverpool City Institute of Further Education

Pitman Publishing

First Published 1972

Sir Isaac Pitman and Sons Ltd
Pitmna House, Parker Street, Kingsway, London WC2B 5PB
PO Box 46038, Portal Street, Nairobi, Kenya

Sir Isaac Pitman (Aust) Pty Ltd
Pitman House, 158 Bouverie Street, Carlton, Victoria 3053, Australia

Pitman Publishing Company SA Ltd
PO Box 11231, Johannesburg, South Africa

Pitman Publishing Corporation
6 East 43rd Street, New York, 10017, USA

Sir Isaac Pitman (Canada) Ltd
495 Wellington Street West, Toronto 135, Canada

The Copp Clark Publishing Company
517 Wellington Street West, Toronto 135, Canada

Paperback edition ISBN: 0 273 36115 5
Cased edition ISBN: 0 273 31487 4

Printed in Great Britain at the Pitman Press, Bath
G2 (G4650/G4620: 15)

Contents

1

Introductory

GENERAL OBJECTIVES

This book aims:

1 To define the essential tasks of the teacher.
2 To relate the basic principles of learning to methods of preparing, presenting and illustrating teaching material.
3 To provide ways of organizing and assessing students' activities.
4 To illustrate methods of both limiting teaching objectives and extending beyond subject boundaries.
5 To point up the social skills and interpersonal relationships involved in teaching.
6 To provide some methods of assessing teacher effectiveness and of self-assessment.

TARGET READERSHIP

Countless untrained part-time and full-time teachers, experienced in their teaching subjects, are responsible for influencing classes in Colleges of Further Education, Evening Institutes, HM Services, Industry, Business and Public Service. This book is for them.

It should meet the requirements of students preparing for the Further Education Teacher's Certificate (Scheme 394) of the City and Guilds of London Institute; and for the Teacher's Certificates in Shorthand, Typewriting and Office Practice of the Royal Society of Arts.

BACKGROUND

This book is the result of the author's experience during twenty years' teaching "on the shop floor", and of observing, advising and assessing a thousand teachers in classroom, craftroom, workshop, laboratory, garage, kitchen, surgery, clinic, office, field, mine, prison, public house, church, on stage and aboard ship. The material has been tried out on these teachers and is the result of many shifts and changes in dynamic learning situations.

Indirectly my colleague, Donald Hurst, and many students have contributed through discussion, criticism and performance to the ideas and tone of the book.

2

Further Education

RESPONSIBLE BODIES AND TEACHING ESTABLISHMENTS

The term "Further Education" refers to the courses, tuition, instruction and learning, full-time and/or part-time, of persons who have left school. Further Education extends from the statutory school-leaving age to well beyond the state pensionable age of 65. It embraces vocational courses, non-vocational courses and recreational classes. Much of this education is provided in institutions maintained or aided by local education authorities: polytechnics, National Colleges (which provide advanced courses for specialized technologies), colleges of technology, technical colleges, colleges of further education, colleges of art, colleges of building, colleges of commerce, other monotechnics (e.g. colleges of food, fashion, distributive trades), adult colleges, and evening institutes.

Some of these institutions provide "Higher Education", i.e. courses leading to degrees or similar qualifications; others offer "Adult Education" (sometimes referred to as OFE or Other Further Education) for students pursuing mainly non-vocational courses. Fig. 2.1 gives an outline of the Further Education system:

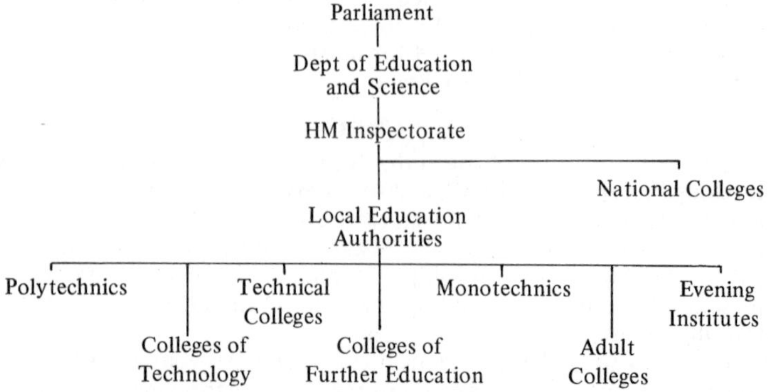

Fig 2.1 *Controlling bodies and the Establishments of Further Education*

There is, however, a vast area of post-school education which is not provided by the institutions already listed, nor by the extra-mural departments of the universities or voluntary bodies such as the Workers' Educational Association (WEA). Much of this education has clear-cut vocational aims and is presented in courses as various as those associated with the colleges of further education — full-time (including sandwich courses), part-time, block-release and day-release, short induction courses, "off-the-job" courses, post-experience courses, refresher courses, and retraining courses. Any attempt to chart this territory of tertiary education would inevitably omit some sectors of activity but the following indicates a number of the main providers:

1 The Industrial Training Boards (ITBs) with their Training Centres and Units
2 Industrial and Commercial Associations and individual employers, who run their own staff colleges and training schools
3 Independent colleges and schools, e.g. for secretarial courses, shorthand and typing; cookery and needlework
4 Correspondence colleges, e.g. National Extension College
5 Schools of Nurse Training
6 Ancillary Medical Schools, e.g. of radiography, occupational therapy, speech therapy
7 The Services, at their academies and training units
8 Music and Drama Schools
9 Theological Colleges

Certain government departments are responsible for many of the courses which they conduct either separately or in conjunction with the Department of Education and Science, often making use of the staff and facilities of colleges of further education.

Fig. 2.2 gives some idea of the complexity of Further Education not directly controlled by the Department of Education and Science.

EMERGENCE

The Education Act of 1944 committed Local Education Authorities "to secure the provision of adequate facilities for further education, including 'leisure-time occupations, in such organised, cultural, training and recreative activities as are suited to their requirements, for any persons over compulsory school age who are able and willing to profit by the facilities provided for that purpose'". The Act reflected the wartime dissatisfaction with (1) the inadequate provision for training craftsmen, technicians and technologists; (2) poorly housed technical

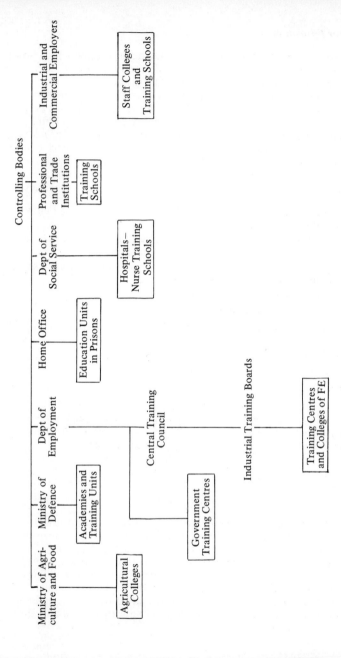

Fig 2.2 *Other controlling bodies and their Establishments of Education and Training*

colleges which were based mainly on evening study; (3) insufficient means of satisfying the appetite for cultural and recreational adult education.

The growth of post-elementary education was slow to develop after the Education Act of 1870, which saw the beginning of the maintained and rate-aided system of public education in this country. The pattern of technical and commercial education was based mainly upon part-time evening study until the second world war. By 1905 there were about three-quarters of a million students attending evening classes and from that time until 1938 Education Committees provided continuing education, with little central guidance. "Under pressure from parents to provide relevant education for a skilled job for their children, from industrialists to furnish the technical background required by their employees, and from commerce to train typists, book-keepers and other staff with specific skills, county borough authorities developed technical and commercial education on an *ad hoc* basis during the first fifty years of this century. Technical and commercial colleges worked under every handicap imaginable: scattered in numerous buildings (often disused schools), starved of finance and staffed with personnel whose status and qualifications were uncertain, they nevertheless endeavoured to meet local demands as best they could."[1]

EXPLOSION

An explosion of further education occurred in the fifties, following the publication of the government White Paper *Technical Education* (1956). Since that time substantial capital projects have been implemented. The main weight of classes has switched from part-time evening to part-time day classes and then, in terms of teaching hours, to full-time day classes in the sixties. Consumer demand, sometimes backed by Government policy, has led to the rapidly growing tendency for school-leavers either to take "A" level and other school subjects, or full-time courses at colleges of further education or to go to employment and part-time further education.

Following the publication of the White Paper *Better Opportunities in Technical Education* (1961) emphasis has been placed upon the provision of courses for technicians. One consequence has been the action of the professional institutions involved in the Council of Education Institutions (CEI): in recognizing the gradation of the various levels of skill required in industry, they have decided to withdraw recognition of courses of part-time study as an appropriate route

[1] George Taylor *Trends in Education,* 1870 Centenary Issue (page 44). (1970, HMSO)

to the professional status of a chartered engineer. The Haslegrave Report (1969) on the training of technicians advocates the possibility of bridging courses to fill the gap between the technician, the technician engineer and the chartered engineer of the institutions.

The Industrial Training Act of 1964 aimed at improving the quality and efficiency of personnel at all levels in industry and commerce. This enabled the establishment of Industrial Training Boards (ITBs) for each of the major industries. In densely populated industrial areas the ITBs have often utilized the colleges of further education for "off-the-job" training and integrated courses of education and training. Nevertheless, in rural areas classes are often not viable because of insufficient numbers of students, and small firms sometimes opt to pay a levy to the ITB and do little or no training of their workers.

Following the 1966 White Paper *A Plan for the Polytechnics and other Colleges* about thirty polytechnics offering higher education at degree level have been formed from existing regional colleges and other colleges. Some of these polytechnics, which have responsibilities mainly for full-time students but also for part-time courses including both refresher and post-experience courses, are starting by being larger than some present-day universities.

PROBLEMS

Controversies exist. The principal problems concern:

1 The lack of co-ordination between the upper reaches of secondary education and less advanced further education.
2 Failure to decide whether further education is a national or a local service.
3 The dual system of higher education in (*a*) the public sector, the polytechnics and other area colleges and (*b*) the university sector.
4 The respective parts to be played in non-vocational adult education by local education authorities, universities and voluntary organizations.
5 The desirability of integrating education and training under a new Department of Education, Science and Training.

The demands for trained manpower for technologically advanced industries in time of war, the necessity to increase the productivity and profitability of industrial and commercial enterprise in the postwar world, and the insatiable demand for more continuing and higher education are the main socio-economic factors which have effected the large-scale development of further education in its different forms — vocational, cultural and recreative.

FURTHER DEVELOPMENT

Post-school education is likely to expand in response to:

1 The extension of full-time education of young people.
2 Further implementation of the Industrial Training Act (1964), aimed at improving the quality and efficiency of personnel at all levels in industry and commerce.
3 The need for re-training to keep pace with technological change.
4 The growing demand for leisure and recreational pursuits.
5 The increased awareness of the need for preparation for retirement.

FURTHER READING

L Cantor and I F Roberts *Further Education in England and Wales,* 1969, Routledge, Kegan Paul (pages 1–41)

Education for the Future, ATTI January 1970 (13 pages). From the Association of Teachers in Technical Institutions, Hamilton House, Mabledon Place, London WC1N 9BH

3

Teaching in Further Education

Teaching is an art. Viewed as an art, teaching need never be dull. It is something to be practised, not merely known; something to be improved, refined, perfected. A teacher can best acquire and improve his power to teach by teaching. Every time he presents a topic he should vary the emphasis and detailed handling of the material in response to the students. In this way a skill is acquired — the ART OF TEACHING.

THE TEACHING SITUATION

Whether the teacher faces an individual student or a small group or a large class, in the model office or in the kitchen, in the laboratory or on the building site, the teaching is energized from three distinct focal points — the teacher (T), the student (S) and the teaching material (M) involved in the activity. The success of the teaching is the outcome of the interaction of these three factors:

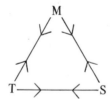

Fig 3.1 *The teaching situation*

TEACHER EDUCATION

Education in the art of teaching should always be accompanied by practice; indeed a training course *after* a teacher has been at work for some time is most valuable, though in a perfect world no one would be allowed to teach without some preliminary training, accompanied by supervised practice.

In England and Wales much Technical, Business, Defence and Social Service education is in the hands of teachers who have not been professionally trained. The subject matter of Further Education is in many instances at the disposal of only those who are or have been engaged in industry, business and military, social and domestic services. These teachers start with the advantage of knowledge acquired in the most effective way – by practice.

In their employment these teachers have often been accustomed to having their tasks defined in terms of a desired result and a period for its completion; in relation to the resources available and environment provided. Their progress might have been monitored and controlled to ensure a satisfactory result. In Further Education the teacher's goals and techniques need not be a matter for conjecture. There is a body of facts and theories about how to teach and about how and why students learn.

The ordered body of knowledge, accumulated by educational psychology, the science related to the art of teaching, will repay study. Teaching requires practice of the tasks essential in most organizations:

1 Setting goals and objectives (appropriate to the needs and expectations of the students).
2 Choosing the methods most effective in achieving these goals.
3 Checking and assessing performance, results and effect.

A wide range of equipment is available to the majority of teachers, although there is sometimes a lack of suitable materials to use with the "hardware" of cine-projectors, recording machines, teaching machines, language laboratories, overhead projectors, computers and closed circuit television. The teacher's art lies in the selection of materials and media suited to the needs of his students. He should be aware of the widening range of modern techniques of communication and their potential value.

Class teaching remains the chief form of teaching in Further Education. There are, however, increasing instances of the teacher's forming part of a team of teachers, who are responsible for the learning activities of students either in large groups or small groups or individually. Even if the scheme of work has been prepared by a team of teachers, the individual teacher remains responsible for the presentation of his own lessons, which he prepares within the limits of his time and resources. Not even the most sophisticated computer can achieve the degree of delicate adjustment which a good teacher can achieve in meeting the precise needs of his students.

He will mount his teaching/learning initiatives with regard to the attitudes, learning procedures and memory strategies acquired by his students in earlier stages of formal education and nurtured through perpetual use.

It is encouraging to read in the early literature of the Open University[1] that it seeks in its part-time tutors a willingness to learn with the student. In every teaching situation in further education the teacher should be the most conspicuous learner. The education of the teacher (self-promoted and perpetuated) should be seen as a continuous process, being concerned with the development and management of learning situations; the analysis of problems stemming therefrom; the constant objective reappraisal of self and one's interactions with others.

Courses of teacher education are not sufficient in themselves. They should be supplemented by contact with teachers in their classes and by the teachers themselves in contact with other teachers — particularly those taking the same or similar subjects. The advantages of training accrue to both teacher and his students:

1 *To the students*
(a)   There will be a scheme of work suited to their abilities and interests.
(b)   They will be making the best use of their time.
(c)   Their efforts will be evaluated and justified by their achievement.

2 *To the teachers*
(a)   A job they are interested in is made more enjoyable and rewarding.
(b)   Confidence in the ability to teach well is acquired in a time much shorter than if learning were confined to general trial and error and experience only.
(c)   It is reassuring to find that techniques discovered by the teachers themselves are effective or need little improvement.

LECTURERS OR TEACHERS

In Further Education teachers are styled as lecturers or instructors or tutors. Teaching periods are usually called lectures. A lecture can be recorded on tape without a class being present, and played to a group of students. A lesson requires the students to take part — not just listen but answer and pose questions and join in discussion. To be effective the lecture should be supplemented by directed private reading, exercises, discussion periods and tutorials. Time is at a premium in most courses and consequently the lecture or uninterrupted exposition by the teacher should be used with discretion, if there is little time for supplementary teaching methods. A lesson, which will include provision for a variety of student activity and

[1] *Further particulars for Part Time Tutors,* May 1970, The Open University

make use of a number of teaching techniques, will generally be more appropriate. In making a choice between lecture and lesson, the teacher should be guided by his knowledge of the intellectual skills at the disposal of the learners, and of the level of language at which the recipients are operating.

ESSENTIAL TASKS

The teacher's concern is with conveying facts, ideas, skills and attitudes to his students:

T	Facts	Skills	Attitudes	Ideas	S

Fig 3.2 *Transmission*

The teacher is a facilitator, organizer and supervisor of his students' learning. He is more than a subject expert. His essential tasks are —

SELF-ORGANIZATION: advancing his subject-knowledge, keeping up-to-date; having regard to his dress, speech and outlook on life

SUBJECT-ORGANIZATION: review of syllabus content, correlation with the schemes of colleagues, preparation of schemes of work; lesson organization, preparation of teaching material

METHODS ORGANIZATION: choice of appropriate medium of instruction; a balanced approach appealing to as many senses as possible

ORGANIZATION OF STUDENTS' WORK: setting course work assignments, exercises, projects; testing progress; recording progress

The teacher's activities include the selection, organization and presentation of teaching material but his main responsibility lies in the effective control of the students' learning. He should keep the individual student's development centrally in mind whilst exercising a controlled use of a variety of learning situations which could include a selection of: lesson (or lecture), tutorial, film, teaching machine, practical problem, textbook, reference library, project, laboratory (or workshop or craftroom) periods, free group discussion, case study, role-playing, educational visit, educational television and radio.

DUTIES OF A FULL-TIME TEACHER IN FURTHER EDUCATION

During the 30 hours each week a teacher is on duty, he/she will be occupied in a wide range of activities which may be broadly divided into three main groups.

The first group is usually classified as "class contact hours," which may include indirect work with students as well as directly taking a class. Such duties may include:

1 Invigilating and supervising examinations.
2 Tutorial work with individual students or groups (both inside and outside the college).
3 Supervision of students' research projects.
4 Conducting correspondence courses.
5 Taking students on industrial and educational visits.
6 Participating in residential courses.

The second group of duties may also be considered as necessarily part of the responsibility of a teacher, but the amount of responsibility may vary with the level and nature of the appointment. These duties include:

1 Timetabling.
2 Supervision of courses and classes.
3 Supervision of workshops, laboratories, specialist rooms and ancillary staff.
4 Organizing short courses, residential courses, industrial and educational visits.
5 Special duties such as welfare of students, safety, publicity, liaison with students' union and supervising extra-curricular activities.
6 Special preparation for new techniques in teaching, such as preparing courses of instruction in programmed learning, tapes for language laboratories, programmes for closed circuit television.
7 Liaison work with schools, other colleges, and local industry; advisory services to intending students; and public relations work.
8 Development of new courses, including schemes and syllabuses.

The third group may be described as ancillary duties covering marking, preparation for classes and the keeping of such records of students as a teacher may be reasonably expected to maintain in his professional capacity. Teachers should not normally be engaged in duties which can be performed by ancillary staff, e.g. clerical, laboratory, workshop and library staff. Adequate ancillary services should be made available so that teachers may perform their duties efficiently.

FURTHER READING

Two articles: (i) "Continuing Education" by J A R Pimlott (pages 50–55); (ii) "Towards the Programmed Teacher" by Martyn Clemans (pages 67–70), in *Trends in Education* (February 1970), 1870 Centenary Issue, Department of Education and Science, HMSO

W E Styler *Further Education: Part-time Teachers Speak,* 1968 (33 pages), (Department of Adult Education, University of Hull)

Teaching as Equals, 1969 (141 pages), BBC

4

Students

Teachers exist for the benefit of students. In recent years teaching
has reflected changes in thinking about the role of students, and
teacher-student relations. Part-time vocational courses, in particular,
could until the early sixties be likened to the bed of Procrustes, the
robber who entertained travellers and made them fit the bed in his
guest room by stretching the short ones and trimming down the tall
ones. Few escaped without mutilation. There has been a shift of
emphasis to student-centred teaching, based upon the general capacity,
needs and aspirations of the students.

Post-school education caters for more than three million students
in establishments of further education; in addition vast numbers are
undergoing post-experience courses and spells of re-training conducted
by employers and staff trainers. It spans more than forty years in the
ages of its students. It encompasses an infinite variety and disparity in
the abilities, attainments, occupations, ambitions, goals and domestic
circumstances of its students.

THE ADOLESCENT STUDENT (15—18)

The first day at work or at college is often referred to as the "Death
of a Schoolboy." The school-leaver's first impressions may be long-
lasting. Introductions to their supervisors and teachers provide a useful start in using the first days effectively.

Some education authorities permit students under the statutory
school-leaving age to attend a college of further education on linked
courses, to make use of facilities and accommodation not available at
the school and to experience the more adult atmosphere of the college.
This arrangement gives the student a better prospect of continuing
their studies after leaving school.

With the school-leaving age raised to 16, certain of the recom-
mendations made in the Newsom Report, *Half our Future,* may be
implemented:

1 Lengthening the working day and working month.
2 Introducing homework and directed activities after school hours.

3 Making the final year more practical, realistic, vocational and
   catering for students' choices.

   The transition from school to college could be made smoother if
there were a two-way traffic between staff of the further education
college and the school. The school could prepare students for further
education by:

1 Giving a full five-year general education.
2 Encouraging a more independent approach to studies (instruction
   in note-making, and in using libraries).
3 Increasing the proportion of teachers with industrial and business
   experience.
4 Giving accurate information about the colleges of further education.
5 Holding meetings between school-leavers and college teachers.
6 Providing a planned programme of vocational guidance.
7 Arranging courses of introduction to further education.

   "Leaving School" is too often, in the minds of students and
parents, a final stage, whereas it should be seen as a step in a process
in which further education is a natural continuation of primary and
secondary education. Teachers at colleges of further education, for
their part, could assist students during this period of transition if:

1 The consolidation of school work were presented a fresh way.
2 There were no sharp change in teaching method. Too often, and
   misguidedly the college teacher poses as a pundit on his subject,
   dispensing chalk, talk and dictation as a general practitioner
   prescribing medicine, with the unctuous claim that it is unpalatable
   but good for his patients.
3 The college prospectus – the majority are dreary collations – were
   replaced by more attractive and readable information.

SELECTION FOR COURSES

One of the student's basic needs is to make a wise initial choice of
course. Selection of students should be based upon factors which can
be assessed and are relevant to the job for which they are being
assessed. Colleges, largely from lack of staff trained in guidance and
counselling, have not been remarkably successful in the placement of
students in appropriate courses. The industrial training manager
usually wants not so much a certificate from a school-leaver as
information about his attainments, his "background of opportunity".

   The most widely used guide to selection is the "Seven Point Plan",
which could assist the college teacher as well as the industrial selector

or trainer or interviewer. It provides a useful list of some of the factors which influence individual differences and resemblances in students; it helps in compiling a profile of the student's attainments and his capacity to learn. The plan gives a heading for each of the seven points and key questions for the teacher to ask himself.

THE SEVEN POINT PLAN

I *Physical characteristics*
1 Has he any defect or disability of occupational importance?
2 How impressive are his appearance, bearing and speech?

II *Attainments (and previous experience)*
3 What type of education has he had?
4 How well has he done educationally?
5 What occupational training and experience has he had, if any?
6 How well has he done occupationally?

III *General intelligence*
7 What is the level of his general intelligence?
8 How effectively does he use it?

IV *Special aptitudes*
9 Has he any marked aptitude for understanding mechanical things?
10 Is he good at doing jobs with his hands?
11 Does he express himself easily, in speech and writing?
12 Is he good at figures?
13 Does he draw well?
14 Has he musical talent?

V *Interests*
15 Has he intellectual interests?
16 Has he practical-constructional interests?
17 Has he physically-active interests?
18 Has he social interests?
19 Has he artistic interests?

VI *Disposition*
20 How acceptable does he make himself to other people?
21 Does he influence others?
22 Is he steady and dependable?
23 Is he self-reliant?

VII *Circumstances*
24 What are his domestic circumstances?
25 What do the other members of the family do for a living?
26 Are there any special openings available for him?

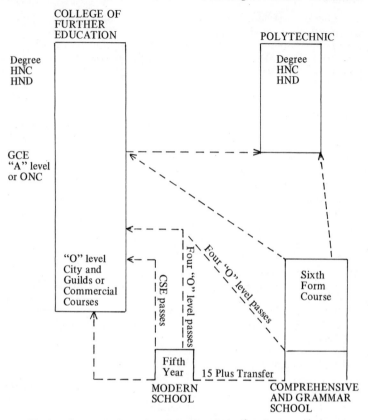

Fig 4.1 *Courses in Secondary Schools and the links between these and
courses in Further Education*

SCHOOL–WORK–COLLEGE

School-leavers are in a period of transition from one environment to
another. The transition may be associated with (1) loss of individual
importance and (2) more onerous conditions, longer hours, and
fewer opportunities for "play". At college no less than at the place
of employment, it is necessary to absorb the students into the new
environment, to explain what services the college provides, how their
courses relate to their personal and vocational needs, what they can
expect from their courses.

Student wastage, in the sense of those who drop out from courses, stems from poor selection, a variety of outside influences, poor teaching, dated and inappropriate syllabuses. These reasons point to the desirability of making the teaching interesting and relevant.

The most observable difference between students in the 15−18 age group is that some attend college willingly or by choice, whereas others attend because it is a condition of their employment. There are also remarkable differences in the rate at which students mature and at which they come to grips with the four major adjustments of:

1 Finding a satisfactory job.
2 Finding a mate.
3 Finding a set of values or standards.
4 Finding acceptance or a niche in employment and in community.

Within this age group the main qualities or differences are those of physique, academic development and intelligence.

1 Physique

Boys vary more than girls in the rate at which they mature. With some boys, teachers cannot be certain that puberty has been reached before the age of 18. However, practical and theoretical tasks are usually related to the student's age rather than his physical development. Standard exercises and equipment are prescribed regardless of physical capacity. Boys are particularly subject to "learning fatigue". This may be mental and muscular resulting from arduous practical exercises or complex theoretical studies. A change of activity may improve this situation and this may be achieved by (1) moving from theory to practice, (2) moving from routine work to an activity that introduces a change, gives variety to the session, (3) moving to a job that exercises different muscles, e.g. from filing to chipping.

Contrary to popular opinion the internal changes of boys between 16 and 19 are usually greater than those of girls. It would appear regrettable that colleges and employers prefer to provide for a special "feminine type of education", on the assumption that there are specifically female qualities, interests and jobs. At this stage girls are physically equipped to enter non-traditional courses leading to an employment as technicians and technologists in industry and commerce.

2 Academic Development

Fig 4.1 shows the links between courses in secondary schools and courses in Further Education. Academic development is generally thought to be measured by performance in examinations, principally of the General Certificate of Education (GCE) and the Certificate of Secondary Education (CSE). Frequently, however, examination results are used to assess: (*a*) a sample of the students' performance in a particular subject, (*b*) the students' capacity or potential to perform well on a course in further education, (*c*) whether the student has reached his "ceiling" level of performance.

Subject passes may not predict with any accuracy a student's success in courses in further education. There are two main routes of study in further education: the academic route (e.g. GCE "A" or OND Business Studies) and the practical-technical route (e.g. City and Guilds, Fabrication of Steel). The secondary school concentrates on providing a general education. It has not been demonstrated that the tasks objects and events in examination courses at school are necessarily relevant to the abilities likely to be called into play in further education courses. For instance, "Metalwork" and "Homecrafts" have different meanings on different examination certificates. Moreover, a "pass" in English does not ensure that the student is able to read discriminatively or write clearly. More important can be the information as to whether the student has had the background of opportunity to develop abilities which will be required in the employment or studies he undertakes after leaving school. A personal interview can provide a useful check upon school reports and examination results.

Most courses in further education require at the minimum level an ability to write a few sentences and perform simple calculations. The majority of young workers need to cope with instructions and information, written, typewritten, duplicated, printed, and spoken, with or without diagrams and graphs. Most technical and scientific and commercial courses have examinations which assess performance in English to some extent. Consequently considerable numbers of students enter upon further education in need of remedial teaching in English. An unconscionable number of young people enter penal establishments unable to read and write. The methods used for teaching sub-literates have some application in a wide range of courses at the colleges:

1 At first dissociate the idea of reading from the idea of books.
2 Stress the more practical uses of reading in connection with the student's own practical interests.
3 Start by exciting interest with advertisements, television announcements, racing news, football results, signs, tickets, announcements in shops and streets, official notices and papers.

The Industrial Training Boards through their own training courses and the courses of integrated training and further education at the colleges are succeeding (where the 1944 Education Act failed) in ensuring that adolescents employ the "tools" of reading and writing acquired at school and so easily allowed to fall into disuse.

3 Intelligence

Intelligence is now viewed as "a set of developed skills with which a person copes with any environment"; and a fundamental skill is learning how to learn. It may be reassuring to be told by researchers that most students will master any task or solve any problem provided they are given sufficient time. But further education courses are rarely flexible enough to allow teachers to train their students in the skills of learning and to allow students as much time as they want and need for learning a subject. Students do not possess just one intellective quality; at least five qualities should be considered in arriving at a picture or "profile" of a student's intelligence:

1 General capacity (flexibility and rapidity of learning)
2 Verbal-educational skills (involving the use and comprehension of written and spoken words
3 Numerical skills (involving the use and comprehension of numerical symbols)
4 Spatial skills (visualizing how an object would look if its spatial position were changed; and also detecting accurately the spatial arrangement of objects with respect to one's own body)
5 Mechanical skills (the ability to see how mechanical objects work and how to make them work)

A student's performance on a standardized test of each of these five "qualities" or categories builds up a profile which gives a comparison of his rate of development in each category. A student who has a high score on a test of mechanical skills may have a low score in a test of verbal skills. But it is folly to place much faith in the dictum, "strong in the arm, therefore thick in the head". No such "law of compensation" has been proved. Above all, no one technique of assessment can be relied upon to establish how intelligent a student is; no one test can measure the whole range of skills of which he is capable.

THE YOUNG ADULT (19–25)

There is an accelerating demand for vocational and general education from young people who have reached the age of majority. In the main students in the age group 19–25 will be following courses leading to a professional qualification or degree courses or other advanced courses, such as Higher National Diploma or Certificate courses of a practical rather than academic type.

Many of the students enter polytechnics and colleges of further education to pursue degree courses (either of the Council for National Academic Awards (CNAA) or the London University external) as a second choice after failing to obtain a place at a university. A substantial number of young people do not want to go to a university (although offered a place there) but prefer another kind of institution. In some cases young people have been advised to go to non-university institutions because it was thought that they would be happier and likely to be more successful there. However, one of the most disturbing situations in "Higher Education within Further Education" is the drop-out of a high percentage of students. "They could be called aspirers rather than achievers." Too often colleges admit students with an inflated sense of their own abilities, with the slenderest of entry qualifications, and without the personal qualities that make for success in a disciplined course of study.

At certain levels, some subjects (e.g. photographic technology) are available only at colleges outside the universities. Students are being attracted by courses which are designed to bring together apparently unrelated subjects such as chemistry with business studies. Such courses may well attract students who prefer a wider range of study or who like both arts and science subjects.

A considerable number of CNAA degree courses are sandwich courses which may require that up to half of the course time may be spent in industrial work related to academic studies. Consequently a high proportion of sandwich-course students are industry-based, employed by firms, and return to the firm for the industrial training period. This arrangement may have the advantage of bridging the gap between the unreality of academic studies and the industrial scene.

MATURE STUDENTS

Further education is showing an increasing interest in providing easy access to vocational training, general educational refreshment and leisure courses for mature students. There are many areas from which students will be drawn, and one of the important attractions is that the courses can be taken without necessarily disrupting any well established pattern of living:

1 Those born too soon to benefit from the increased opportunities provided in recent years
2 Those in professional occupations who wish to attain the status conferred by the award of a degree
3 Those who left school at the minimum leaving age and have the ability to pursue an academic course

4 Those women whose maturing attitudes incline them towards study for personal satisfaction or betterment

Retraining

Changes in technology, the de-skilling of crafts, the decimalization of the currency, the introduction of a metric system of measurement, the emergence of new skills — all these factors produce a need for re-training older workers. Many will assume the role of trainee or student long after leaving school. Older workers exhibit certain broad characteristics in their learning —

1 They prefer a method of teaching where there is a free flow of information and attitudes and ideas between students and students and between teacher and students.
2 They are suspicious, sometimes resentful, of a "chalk and talk" session, which may have painful associations with failure experienced in earlier years.
3 They feel happier when their learning is not "paced", when they are without the stress of a time test.
4 They gain confidence when the amount of learning is strictly limited and "correct" learning is ensured in easy stages.
5 They assimilate new material and retain it better when it is presented in terms of situations and problems which they already appreciate.

Non-vocational

Adults who pursue non-vocational courses make up a sizeable proportion of the students in further education. They attend courses either because they want to *do* things for themselves or because they want a better service from those who do things for them. A teacher of "Car Maintenance" finds that his students at one evening institute wish to save money by doing repair jobs themselves, whereas students in another area attend because they wish to learn whether they receive satisfactory service at their garage.

It is in adult classes that the least effort is made at selection and grading of students. Students attend voluntarily: if they are dissatisfied with what they receive they "vote with their feet". It is not unusual for a teacher of shorthand to have a class in which absolute beginners sit alongside intermediate and advanced students. The student's wants may often differ from their needs. The student of dress may *want* to make a garment but may first *need* to know how to make a button-hole.

Most adults take their classes in one short burst and only a small proportion of students return to classes after an interval. In recent

times adult education has suffered from periods of financial strin-
gency. Some students of ballroom dancing and physical recreation
have found that their education authority has discriminated against
those more "frivolous" classes and closed them.

Prisoners

Short-stay and long-term inmates of prisons and other penal establishments were the object of over 200,000 classes organized in 1967. The
policy of the Prison Department is to link Education Officers in all
penal establishments with the mainstream of education through
Colleges of Further Education. A policy statement of 1969 stressed
a clear need for programmes to reflect education "as a tool for a job,
an aid to living, and to frame them within adult rather than school
outlines". In the near future certain inmates with potentially good
intellectual capabilities may need full-time education and vocational
training linked with Colleges, and related to keeping alive the prisoner's
sense of well-being and usefulness to society.

Preparation for Retirement

As the expectation of life increases and with it the proportion of the
population who are approaching or have reached the age of retirement, so there will be larger numbers of people seeking education
for retirement. Some work-people will never before have been students
most will be unaccustomed to formal and systematic study. Often
they will be anxious about the changes to be made in their daily
routine, adjustments in financial and housing arrangements, how to
use new-found leisure hours. A six-week course arranged on a day-
release basis for men on the brink of retirement has followed this
programme of discussions and demonstrations. (See Fig. 4.2.)

FURTHER READING

A Rodger *The Seven Point Plan,* 1952 (16 pages), National Institute of Industrial Psychology

Ethel Venables *The Young Worker at College,* 1967 (240 pages), Faber and
Faber

Education in Prisons, Policy Statement No 1, 1969 (16 pages), Home Office
Prison Department

Alistair Heron *Preparation for Retirement: Solving New Problems,* 1961 (27
pages) From the National Council of Social Service, 26 Bedford Square, London
WC1

WEEK 1	Introduction to the course	"Let's talk about retirement"	Financial Planning Development Officer
WEEK 2	Gardening	Odd jobs in the home	
WEEK 3	Health in retirement	Photography	Holidays
WEEK 4	Why a Welfare Department can help *or* How a Welfare Department can help	Leisure in Retirement	Interior decorating
WEEK 5	Attitudes towards Retirement	How to use your library	
WEEK 6	Housing in retirement – Panel of speakers from – Housing Department Improved Housing Housing Association Building Society	An open forum	Closing session

Fig 4.2 *Preparation for retirement in men*

5
Principles

In this chapter we shall consider why and how students learn, so as to provide a sufficient sub-structure of principles to support our methods of teaching.

LEARNING

It is easier to define the characteristics or attributes of learning than to define *learning* itself. If all learned behaviour were wiped out, a physiologically mature person would be able to do very little – he would be unable to speak, unable to wash and feed himself. As the behaviour of the adult differs greatly from that of a baby, *learning* is the chief cause of this change in behaviour. Changes in behaviour are caused in three ways:

1 By the growth which enables different organs to function properly. This is called *maturation.* For example, changes in behaviour at adolescence, connected with sexual activity, are probably caused by maturation.
2 By physical damage to the organism or *lesion.*
3 By *learning.* All changes other than those due to maturation or lesion must be the result of learning.

Learning produces a relatively permanent change in behaviour.
Learning is not something to be dispensed nor is teaching merely the presentation of information. In other words we cannot equate the teacher's telling with the student's learning. Nor can we judge whether a student has learned without observing some kind of change in his behaviour. We should check whether a student has learned how to bleach hair by observing the student attempting to bleach a client's hair, to see whether the performance is efficient.

Changing our tactics over several attempts to re-ignite the boiler of a gas-fired central heating system would not be classified as learning because we are likely to change tactics again, if they are not successful. Similarly we would not class as learning the preliminary, unsuccessful manœuvres we make when attempting to drive a car. On the other hand, behaviour that leads repeatedly to a successful solution of a problem may be classified as learning. If we are able to re-ignite various gas-fired systems repeatedly, we could consider our behaviour to be evidence of learning.

Learning comes about as a result of practice. If we gradually eliminate our incorrect moves in re-lighting the gas-fired system, we shall have learned to eradicate our mistakes by practice. In this way we learn to act efficiently. However, learning can be depressed when the conditions of practice produce a surfeit of frustration and boredom.

A THEORY OF INSTRUCTION

The teacher new to further education will quickly discover that learning is a voluntary act — students will not be compelled to learn. If we analyse a student's progress in acquiring knowledge of his vocation or subject we can relate it to (1) his desire to learn, (2) his incentive to learn, and (3) his methods of learning. Teaching methods should be chosen in the light of general theory about:

1 Why each student wishes to learn.
2 How this desire to learn may be aroused, maintained and strengthened.
3 The most appropriate means of achieving the aims of the tasks to be undertaken.

The Desire to Learn

This varies widely from person to person. A youth may become an apprentice not because of any wish on his part, but because of parental choice or a teacher's advice. An adult may seek security of employment by obtaining a qualification in engineering, or seek achievement of some academic standard in a foreign language as a form of self-justification within his home or family background. With other students the desire to be competitive, to attain some high standard of performance, or to gain promotion may be the prime drive or motive.

Although students may have various reasons for learning or not wanting to learn, we can discern their basic needs as persons and these should be capitalized. Students need:

1 To enjoy bodily well-being, free physical movement, food and drink, rest and sleep, fresh air.
2 To be accepted and approved, to have personal status in a group.
3 Order and security, routine and system, explanations.

4 Self-esteem; mastery of tasks and skills.

5 To compete against their own standards and those of others; to co-operate with their fellow students.

6 To have new experiences. Often an initial desire to learn is stifled by the teacher spending too much time getting students to memorize facts and too little time making use of his greatest ally, the students' curiosity.

A student's desire to learn will be affected by the aspirations and the atmosphere created by the groups with which he identifies himself, at home, in his locality, at work and at college. Often the intensity of desire will depend on the possible consequences of his learning, whether in the performance of short-term tasks or in readiness to work for distant gratification and future success.

Incentives

At the start of a course of study, the students desire to learn may reveal itself in obvious interest — a tense, eager alertness to the teacher's talk and explanation, a readiness to practise and to follow instructions; anticipation of the next phase in the lesson; and persistent effort towards some goal. Only too frequently a basic desire to learn is insufficient to maintain the full impetus to the learning process over a prolonged period of study or training.

Interest can be initiated and strengthened by positive and negative incentives:

Regular encouragement and approval for effort

Setting intermediate and attainable goals or targets

"Feeling good" in producing a commendable workpiece

Financial rewards

Numerical scores or inspiring commentarial phrases

PRINCIPLES OF LEARNING

During the sixties programmed learning came into vogue. Briefly it is a method of presenting the student with steps or frames of material that is easy to follow, then asking him a question to test his comprehension. The beginning of this chapter might have been written in the style of a so-called "linear" programme. You can test yourself as you go along by sliding a postcard or "mask" down the page as you read.

LINEAR PROGRAMME

1–1	Write on a piece of paper a definition of *learning* before going on to the next frame	
1–2	You will now see how difficult it is to define *learning*. It is easier to discuss the attributes or characteristics of learning. However, keep your definition and look at it later in the light of our discussion	
1–3	B F Skinner, an American "behaviourist" psychologist has indicated that if all *learned* behaviour were wiped out, a mature person would be able to do very little. He would probably find it — to survive	
1–4	Without his learned behaviour, he would be unable to speak, unable to feed himself, unable to wash himself. He would be more like a b— than an adult	1–3 difficult
1–5	Since all normal adults are able to do these things and much more besides, we may say that a very large part of the behaviour of the adult is l—	1–4 baby
1–6	The behaviour of the adult differs greatly from that of the baby. — is the chief cause of this change in behaviour	1–5 learned
1–7	Changes in behaviour may be caused in three ways: 1 By the growth which enables different organs to function properly. This is called *maturation* 2 By physical damage to the organism, or *lesion* 3 By *learning* For example, changes in behaviour at adolescence connected with sexual activity are probably caused by (1) —. Changes in behaviour connected with brain damage are caused by (2) —. All other changes in behaviour must be the result of (3) —	1–6 learning
1–8		1–7 1 maturation 2 lesion 3 learning

Programmes produced in this style may become so dull after a
very short time that students lose all interest in them. Larger frames
of information and more searching questions were often introduced
in later programmes. The most beneficial effect of the programmed
learning movement has been in making teachers aware of how important it is to find out if their teaching method is reaching the intended
goal. In a well designed programme there is an accurate definition of
the aims of the course, the selection of appropriate methods and
materials and media for achieving them, and the testing of these
means to evaluate the success rate.

The secret of the particular success of programmed learning with
teaching mathematics and in industrial and commercial training, lies
in the infinite pains taken to prepare a programme by a programmer
and/or teacher – and also to follow it by the learner. The principles
of programmed learning are not new. They apply to any good teaching method and have long been used by good teachers. The principles
that follow provide an effective method of making us constantly
aware of having an aim and checking whether or not we are reaching
our goal.

Principle 1

*There should be a clear statement of what the student should know
and be able to do at the end of a course or unit of instruction.*

The objectives for a lesson on "Rate of Turnover" in a Commerce
class might read as shown below. Each student should be able to:

1 Calculate the Rate of Turnover for a business.
2 Calculate the basic elements of the Rate of Turnover formula, viz
  Turnover and Average Stock, when given these figures at selling
  price.
3 Exemplify the relationship between rapidity of turnover and the
  profitability of a business.
4 Explain how a business appraises these data in the control of his
  business.
5 Demonstrate why some businesses have a high rate and others
  have a low rate of turnover, and the effect this has on profit
  margins.
6 Distinguish between *turnover* and *rate of turnover.*

The teacher should acquaint his students with the prescribed lesson
objectives and provide them with the experience in which they can
attain these objectives. He should help them work out definite plans
and agree upon some target as this often results in increased performance.

Principle 2

The material to be learned should be relevant to the aims and objectives of the course or unit of learning.

To take an example, if the aim of a course is that students should be able to state the basic make-up of microphones and how each type of microphone operates, it would not be relevant to include a comparison of British and American spelling.

In other words the course content should be selected with reference to the tasks or knowledge we wish our students to demonstrate at the end of their learning. The course would begin with the use and construction of the microphone before continuing with demonstrations and explanations of the crystal microphone and the carbon, ribbon and condenser microphones.

Principle 3

The material should be organized in short, progressive steps in a sequence which is determined by the students' previous knowledge and by their individual needs.

Instruction in "Capacitance", for example, would be organized when it had been confirmed that students have an elementary knowledge of electricity (i.e. should have passed the first year City and Guilds examination in Telecommunications). Fig 5.1 is an example of a sequence of unit steps.

Principle 4

The material should be graded in difficulty so that the student makes few mistakes: the teacher should organize success and minimize failure.

Students will not be able to avoid feeling inadequate and inferior if the tasks we set are too difficult or if they feel they are not progressing. We must break the difficult task down into easy stages, so that each student can succeed in doing them, at the same time not making the steps so easy that the student does not have a sense of achievement.

There is much to be learned from the way in which some industrial trainers organize "job runs", as follows:

1 Analyse the task in detail and break it down into its component parts.
2 Remove anxiety in the trainees by presenting the task in easy stages and providing guide-lines or key points.
3 Make every step relevant and economical.

Basically a capacitor
stores charge

What is charge?

What is the most important
charge (electrically)?

How do charges act?

What factors govern
their action?

Effect of charges
on each other

A capacitor consists
of plates (conductors)
and a dielectric (insulator)

Capacitor
basic action

Construction
and operation

What happens when
an electro-motive force
is connected across
a capacitor?

Effect of emf

Capacitor in
action

How does charge
form on capacitor
plates?

Dependence on
applied voltage

Basic equation
$Q = CV$

Fig 5.1 *Sequence of unit steps*

Our illustration is of a "job run" for hand-packing of "Swish" powder from polythene bags.

HAND-PACKING "SWISH" FROM POLYTHENE BAGS

Stages	*Key points*
1 Preparations – 2 operatives	Place prepared polythene bags of Swish packets on feed end of belt. Empty equally on to No. 1 trays.
2 Inspection and weighing	Take one packet of "Swish", inspect seams for breakage, weigh (reject under weight, pass any up to 2 drams overweight). Place weighed packet on No. 2 tray.
3 Packing "Swish" into box	Take packet from No. 2 tray and place into prepared box, leaving top flap undone. Feed box into guide rails.
3(a) Preparing box for packer	Insert left hand into bottom of flat box, squeeze right side, with right hand to form the box shape. Bend two side flaps with thumbs. Complete base of box by drawing large flaps forward and inserting into box. Place box in storage compartment for packer.
4 Packing finished product into skillet	Pick up flat stamped skillet with writing upside down. Push two narrow flaps in, followed by two wide flaps to make base. Turn skillet right side up smooth base for even packing. Close top flaps of box and pack boxes into skillets in four rows of nine. Close skillet (two narrow flaps first, then two wide flaps). Put skillet on to rollers.

Principle 5

Each student should proceed through a course of learning at his own pace.

If a teacher is teaching one student, it should be possible for him to make each item in the teaching process relate to the previous item and be adapted to the student's needs and capabilities. This situation rarely exists in the classroom. With a class of twenty-four students, it will be impossible for him alone to teach in a way that satisfies the needs of each and every student.

Dr Norman Crowder, the American psychologist, has been primarily interested in using a student's answers to determine and control the order and presentation of teaching material. To attain this control, he

adopts multiple-choice, question-and answer techniques. To return to
our example of "Capacitance" the following snippet illustrates the
Crowderian or "branching" technique of presenting information:

BRANCHING PROGRAMME

Frame	Information
	ELECTRIC CHARGES
1	Try this easy experiment. Tear up some light paper into small pieces and place them on a table top. Rub the shaft of an ordinary plastic ball pen on the hair at the nape of the neck. Provided all the materials are dry, the plastic becomes electrified and will pick up the small pieces of paper.
	This effect is due to *static charges* of electricity.
	When we rub two materials together the ELECTRONS are rubbed off one material on to the other. The PROTONS stay behind. The surplus of electrons on the one material gives it an electric charge we call *negative*. The shortage of *electrons* on the other material means a surplus of *protons* which gives it a *positive* charge.
	Consequently there are two elementary electric charges. Which is the more important electric charge:
	(*a*) the *proton?* – Turn to page 4*a* (*b*) the *electron?* – Turn to page 3*a* (*c*) Neither? – Turn to page 10*b*
4(*a*)	You have said that the *proton* is the more important electric charge. Your answer is not correct. There is a particle which plays a greater part in electric effects. Re-read the introduction on Frame 1, then try again.

The "brighter" student would have turned to page 3*a* and would
probably have continued to work through the programme of instruction at a faster rate.

If teaching in the classroom is designed to teach some "average"
member of a group efficiently, then besides accelerative material for
the "brighter" students, it becomes necessary to provide remedial
material for the "slower" students. This lays stress on the "management" aspect of teaching. It is easier to occupy a group of students
of different abilities than it is to ensure that they are all learning. It
became a source of amazement to observe a French class of a dozen
students, some with a GCE "O" level pass, one with an "A" level pass,
and beginners, who sat next to students who had tried and rejected
classes in "examination" French. The very skilful and sensitive French

teacher kept them all learning at their own rate. But that rate was quickened because the teacher took a hand in seeing that *all*-students were active. It is doubtful whether a student will progress in his studies, if he plays a passive role in regulating his own development. Further departures in programmed learning have led to group viewing of material to be learned, and inevitably to the pacing of learning.

Programmed learning has compelled serious and critical thought about learning and teaching. The American, B S Bloom, has suggested that most children will master any task or solve any problem provided they are given sufficient time. For teachers in further education, needless to say, financially and economically, there just is not time to wait or to provide for some of our students. It is difficult to envisage a time when individual tuition will be provided on such a scale as to cater for all the different learning speeds of students. The alternative would appear to be the redesigning of our educational system as an integrated system, using teachers and machines, mass-instructional media, together with individual tuition, television, films and the library. Such a "system" approach is gradually taking shape.

In the meantime the teacher can attempt to recognize individual differences in rates of learning, by adopting a tactical approach which makes use of class, small group and individual teaching.

Principle 6

The student should be actively involved in the learning process.
If a student wishes to master a subject or skill he needs to make a physical and mental effort:

1 To acquire the knowledge.
2 To retain that knowledge.
3 To put the knowledge to practical use.

Knowledge comes from the processing of experience we gain through the various senses — sight, hearing, touch, taste, smell. In the learning of skills (e.g. touch typing, assembly tasks) the muscular "kinaesthetic" sense is employed. Learning is the process of registering and retaining knowledge.

In practical and technical subjects on the one hand and in discursive studies on the other hand, many teachers are dissatisfied that students have to spend so much time memorizing facts. The majority of students in Further Education are or will be concerned with making things or making things work: with making a victoria sponge, or with cutting pipes to given angles, or with treating cardiac arrest, or lowering a telescopic topmast on a cargo ship, or defrosting a refrigerator. They learn from experience, both physical and mental. They learn by *doing*. The student of housekeeping will learn to use floral décor to the best advantage only by trial and error. Some preliminary theorizing may make this process one of trial and success. However, the student will find out whether the décor is appropriate only by trying out the combinations of colours and forms – by *doing*.

The basic instinct of *curiosity* can be the teacher's greatest ally. Students can be encouraged to explore the visible tools and processes of their subject and trade. Facts learned through new and first-hand experiences tend to remain longer. "Chalk, talk and dictation", however, is still a method too frequently met in colleges and training centres, although often demonstrably unsuited to students. The students' desire to explore has been neglected in the tertiary stage of education. Students want to explore: it involves groping and fumbling and making mistakes. This is how judgement is developed. "Investigations" (of the "why" and "how" of a process) have become more popular with teachers and students of the 16–19 group; the "Discovery" method has found a place in industrial training, particularly in the retraining of older workers. "Discovery" learning has been defined[1] as

Developing understanding through
Involvement in
Special tasks
Challenging and under
Own control:
Venturing and
Exploring is
Remembered and
Yields better results

The teacher's greatest problems arise when he wants his students to come to grips with, to understand, what they can neither see nor touch. Here much of the students' learning derives from second-hand or substitute experience, the teachers' experience, the experience of others from books or similar past experience. The teacher can attempt to use concrete connections but above all must stimulate the imagination, if he wishes his students to grapple with abstract ideas about for example atoms and molecules in science, or triangulation in the Fabrication of Steel, or "liaison" in sauces.

Often it is impossible to provide students with the first-hand experience of seeing, or handling, or hearing, or tasting or smelling, or operating. But there are numerous methods of applying our

[1] R M Belbin *The Discovery Method in Training,* 1969, page 28, Training Information Paper 5, DEP, HMSO

Principle 6 – of involving students in the learning process. Educational practice has moved from a teacher-centred to a student-centred approach. The reactions of the students are more and more widely used. As teaching methods, role play and case study are comparative newcomers in Further Education to questioning, discussion, investigations, practical exercises, experiments and projects. All these methods are now being used to involve students actively in their learning. They will be explained in a later chapter.

Principle 7

The student should receive continual knowledge of how he is progressing throughout the course.

When a student bakes a loaf of bread and submits it to his teacher for comment, "very good" or a similar mark of approval gives the student some indication of how successful he has been. This remark would give minimum *feedback* to the student. To point out the strengths and weaknesses of the loaf in terms of texture, crust, colour, smell and taste would probably be more helpful to the student. To give a percentage mark to the student's effort would be another way of giving the student some knowledge of how well he had done; to show how many marks had been allocated to each observable quality of the loaf would be more likely to help the student in improving his performance. If the teacher fails to comment upon the quality of the loaf, the student is less likely to learn from his mistakes, is less likely to make an effort to improve upon his product.

The delay between the student's completion of a task and assessment from the teacher is often too long. It is also the mark of inefficient teaching. If, when you answer the telephone, you never heard anyone's voice, your answering the phone would not be *reinforced* and you would eventually stop answering it. Success in learning is reinforcing, that is it encourages the student to repeat his successful behaviour. To return to the example of the student who baked the loaf, the teacher's remark "very good" fulfils two functions; it provides knowledge of results and also provides reinforcement, since the activity it follows is successful. Assessment and feedback are integral parts of the learning process. The teacher should base his teaching initiatives upon his analysis of these two components.

Ideally a student should receive a progress report or comment after the learning or performance of each step in a task. If he has to wait until his loaf has been baked he might have made mistakes which could have been rectified earlier, if he had been given continual appraisal of his work. Both final evaluation of the loaf and concurrent appraisal of the student's efforts are important in supplying the student with knowledge of success and of strengthening his learning.

The time lapse between setting a homework exercise to a day-release student or to an evening class student, receiving it a week later and returning it a fortnight after the first date is a frequent occurrence. It is not difficult to see that the student would benefit from a quicker knowledge of results.

Principle 8

The student should master each unit of material before continuing with the next.

To master a subject a student needs:

1 A motive.
2 Time to assimilate the subject matter.
3 The capacity to retain what he has assimilated.

Motive

Without a motive for studying a subject the student's capacity to assimilate and the capacity to retain what he is trying to learn are diminished. Where the student has no *interest* in the subject it is the tutor's duty to help the student develop an interest. He could establish what a student's existing interest is and try to link it up with his subject. The girl who is reluctant to study the theory of hair bleaches, dyes and rinses may be led to see its relevance through her interest in fashion. Students of Navigation have been known to obtain far more correct answers to mathematical problems when the word "ship" has appeared in the wording of the problem.

The teacher by his own interest in his subject can excite an interest in the student, perhaps by his references to his own investigations or industrial experiences. Quite often a teacher will so vividly present his subject that the students' interest is aroused. To study a subject for the purpose of passing an examination is not a promising start to generating any lasting interest in the subject. However, many an engineering student obliged to study English to comply with the regulations of his institution, has quickly realized the help it gives him in the writing of reports.

Without interest concentration is impossible. Interest increases the length of time a student can, without interruption, pursue a given task — it increases his SPAN OF ATTENTION. When the student's span of attention is short, the teacher's object should be to organize the student's time so that he has changes of activity and short-term goals to attain.

Assimilation

The student's assimilation of material is a highly selective process. The function of the teacher is to make the student strive to solve a problem or master a skill – to learn DELIBERATELY. But according to his interests and needs the student reacts to only a small part of what is going on around him (his ENVIRONMENT). The student is continually influenced by suggestions and unconsciously imitates behaviour and practices of his teacher and his fellow students (we say that the student learns UNWITTINGLY).

In most subjects there will be a certain amount of material that has to be *learned by heart,* for example, equations, formulae, a list of directions. A student may be introduced to the history of trade unions by repeating a list of dates, or he may learn to solve a problem by repeating the steps demonstrated by the teacher. In both examples knowledge is achieved by repetition. This *learning by rote* is a method that may be used when intelligent thought and deduction are not required or are not possible.

It is also common practice to use initial letters (ROYBIV to recall the colours of the spectrum – Red, Orange, Yellow, Blue, Indigo and Violet) or "catch phrases" or mnemonics ("Pose, Pause and Pounce" as a recipe for class questioning.) Students of nursing and the medical sciences find these kinds of aids useful.

It is hardly profitable to try to learn by heart material which is understood only imperfectly. It is better for the teacher to arrange new material – facts and ideas – in a systematic way, so that the relations between the facts and the ideas are easily grasped. Meaningful learning results from linking up new learning with existing knowledge.

Retention

Students remember more easily material that has been linked to what they already know, they remember detailed facts of a subject that have been organized into a simplified form.

A student can find out whether he has mastered a unit of subject matter through being questioned, tested, and given oral and written drills. Manual skill can be developed by practice until it becomes habitual.

Periodic revision as well as frequent use and application of the newly acquired material will aid retention. It is not sufficient for the student to acquire and master each unit of material before continuing with the next. He should revise or relearn the material, since memories of what he has learned fade with the passage of time unless refreshed or reactivated. It is not, however, merely repetition which is a valuable aid to retention — the vitally important activity is that concerned with the successful application and exploitation of the new learning as soon as possible following acquisition. Forgetting is to be most expected for knowledge that is not used. How well something is remembered depends upon how well it is learned, on how completely the motor skills or verbal skills have been perceived and assimilated in the first place.

According to the situation three different methods of approach to orthographic projection — the first-angle, the American, and the third-angle — are taught. A student who has learned the first-angle method will frequently find difficulty in acquiring and retaining a second method. The new method competes with the responses the student brings forward from past experience with another method. Interference is obviously to be expected, since the student comes to many topics with partially incorrect ideas. The principal source of forgetting would appear to be the interference between correct interpretations and imperfectly suppressed interpretations.

SUMMARY OF TEACHING PRINCIPLES

1 Define course objectives in terms of what the student should know and be able to do at the end of the course.
2 Make the subject matter relevant to the aims and objectives of a course or unit of instruction.
3 Organize teaching material in progressive steps, determined by the students' knowledge and their individual needs.
4 Grade subject matter so as to organize success and minimize failure.
5 Allow the student to proceed at his optimum rate.
6 Involve the student actively in his learning.
7 Give the student continual knowledge of his progress throughout a course.
8 Ensure that the student masters each unit of teaching material before continuing with the next unit.
9 Organize periodic testing and revision of course work.

FURTHER READING

What is Programmed Learning? 1965 (104 pages) BBC

B M Foss *Education as Art, Science and Technology,* 1967 (28 pages) Harrap

6

Preparation and Planning

It has been known for some teachers of Liberal or General Studies to undertake no preparation for facing their classes beyond taking a copy of a daily newspaper from which they discuss a topic of immediate interest. They may feel that a statement of course content and a prescription of the order in which topics should be taught are contrary to the aims of "liberalizing." They may hold the view that detailed collection of material is not required because of their grasp of the subject matter, and because of their considerable experience of teaching it. Such teachers are not necessarily unsuccessful. Teachers of most subjects will already possess a great deal of necessary information as a result of their own training. What they have to consider is how to make that information available; how, in fact, to help their students to learn. Teachers are guides, who show the best routes. If they are to be effective guides they must study the routes. This is what preparation means. Preparation is of three kinds:

1 Designing or mapping out the work for a course spread over a term or a session
2 Collection and organization of teaching material
3 Planning of each unit of instruction or lesson

PREPARATION OF A COURSE

Most teachers are provided with a syllabus prescribed by an external examining body. However, there is an increasing number of short refresher courses, post-experience courses, and non-vocational courses which are designed by practising teachers themselves. In the first instance the selection of course topics has been made for the teacher, in the second the course teacher will be responsible for determining the ideas, principles and skills involved. Generally teachers have been happier to work to a syllabus laid down by an examining body in spite of two shortcomings of "official" syllabuses: (1) their vagueness; (2) the difficulty of reconciling the dictates of the syllabus with the educational needs of the students and the aims of the training.

Syllabus – Scheme of Work

A syllabus is usually no more than a list of topics to be covered in a
course. A syllabus is usually conceived by an examiner (or examining
body) to indicate the area from which examination or assignments
will be drawn. Rarely does it indicate the relative importance of each
topic, the depth to which each topic should be taught or the order
in which topics should be taught. In arranging his scheme of work the
teacher will find it useful to write each of the topics on a separate
card so that he can arrange them in the best possible teaching sequence.
He should rely upon his experience as a student and on his teaching
experience in arriving at this sequence. There is the story of the new
teacher of science who, having presented his class with his first lesson
of the course, promptly informed his Head of Department that he
had covered all the topics of the syllabus and asked what he should
teach in the next lesson. Unwittingly he had stumbled upon an effective way of starting his scheme of work, by giving a bird's-eye view
of the programme. Very appropriately the HOD advised that the rest
of his course should be taken up with filling in the details of each
topic whilst keeping the whole of the course in view. What is often
referred to as "logical" order is rarely the one which results in the
most effective learning. It is better to arrange topics in an order which
is more likely to interest and challenge the students. The majority of
vocational courses show that theory or principles are interdependent
with processes or practice. When preparing a scheme of work, teachers
should bear in mind this interdependence of their subject with others
and should try to "correlate" their work with that being done in other
subjects and at the place of employment. If the basic sciences taught
are to have any meaning for the medical laboratory student there must
be close liaison between the basic science tutor and the medical science
tutor, whether the latter be college-based oɪ hospital-based. Wherever
possible, working examples given to illustrate principles in basic
sciences should be chosen from the student's day-to-day experience.
Conversely, the medical laboratory tutor, when teaching the use of
new equipment, should bear in mind the scientific principles behind
it and refer directly to them. In order to illustrate how this may be
accomplished, let us consider the ONC syllabuses for Elective Medical
Sciences, in particular the mathematics section. This, in broad terms,
covers the theories of statistics and probability including the use of
calaculation machines and slide-rules. To correlate this syllabus with
the everyday experience of the student, examples should be chosen
from the medical laboratory. For example:

Statistics: frequency of ABO blood groups; establishment of normal
          ranges

Sampling: dilution factors in blood-counting techniques, and relating
    back to whole blood
Distribution: poison distribution in red cell counting

When a syllabus is prescribed by an external examining body the
following steps would prove useful before translating it into a scheme
of work:

1 Look at the syllabus as a whole. For example, the City and Guilds
    course 151 in Cookery for the Hotel and Catering Industry will
    include Related Studies comprising Menu Composition, Food
    Values, Costing, Kitchen Organization and Equipment and Hygiene.
    Integration of professional skills with the principles of trade cookery
    and hygiene will be possible only if a broad view is taken of the
    syllabus, and if collaboration with colleagues is achieved.
2 Study examiners' reports on previous examinations. These are infor-
    mative on the questions that gave most difficulty, and suggestive
    of the amount of time that should be allocated to certain topics of
    the syllabus.
3 Study past examination papers to establish whether there is a good
    coverage of the syllabus and a generous choice of questions, and to
    gauge the difficulty level of the questions.
4 Consult the prescribed list of textbooks and find out whether they
    are readily available and whether they should be supplemented.
5 Calculate the total time available for teaching after allowing time
    for (*a*) tests, (*b*) revision, (*c*) industrial visits, (*d*) demonstrations
    and (*e*) examinations.
6 Ascertain whatever knowledge of a topic students should have
    from previous courses. For example, students on the 151 course
    in Cookery should have acquired a basic knowledge of hygiene in
    their previous course (in Subject 147 or 150).

Course Design
The steps involved in the systematic planning and preparation of a
course are:

1 A statement of what the students should know and be able to do
    at the end of the course.
2 An analysis of the ideas, principles and skills to be taught.
3 A method of assessing the extent to which the students will have
    achieved what they are intended to achieve.

Frequently courses are offered to indeterminate groups of students.
For instance, a spate of courses on decimalization of the currency
has brought together groups of students with widely differing needs

and expectations of the course, as well as disparity in rates of learning, will to concentrate, and linguistic ability.

Courses should be designed (1) for known or specified group of students and (2) to include opportunities of finding out whether the course is producing what it intends to produce and whether it is giving the students what they think is good for them, or what the teacher thinks is good for them. A simple system might be as shown in Fig 6.1

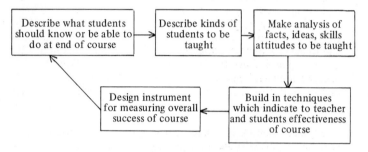

Fig 6.1 *A simple system of designing a course*

Modules

The study programme of the Open University will consist of a number of one-year courses, each leading to the award of a *credit,* if the work is successfully completed. The courses can be taken, if so desired, one at a time over several years with intervals between; a maximum of two courses can be taken in one year. A similar system has operated in the USA and Canada. In this country the Industrial Training Boards have introduced a similar arrangement — the *module,* a self-contained section of a course of study. In a course of study which lasts 48 weeks the syllabus may consist of 8 main topics — 6 weeks x 4 and 12 weeks x 2. Each of these topics is a module. Providing the modules are not progressive, they may be taken in any order. If they are progressive, the order is prescribed.

COLLECTION AND ORGANIZATION OF TEACHING MATERIAL

After compiling a scheme of work, the teacher collects and organizes the material for his teaching. Most teachers will possess a "library of information" composed of lecture notes for courses they have attended more or less recently. In addition they often know their subject matter from personal experience. However, they may not have had recent occasion to retrieve their subject information. The teacher of welding may not have practised his craft with commercial mild steels for many years. He may have difficulty in finding the right sequence of operations in welding vertical or overhead butts: not because he has not known it, nor because he is unable to recognize it when he is presented with it, but because he is unable to recall it. These problems call for relearning of subject matter. Deficiency in the teacher's knowledge must be made good. Next the teacher should ensure that:

1 *Information is technically accurate.*
The fuel technologist might have been solely concerned with fostering co-operation between the motor-car manufacturer and the oil-producing companies in the production of more efficient fuels. He may experience difficulty in giving an *elementary* description of the chemical structure of liquid fuels to motor-vehicle technicians.

2 *Information is up-to-date.*
The teacher of millinery may be convinced that she has a sound knowledge of the psychological implications of colours, but would experience some loss of face if students were to point out repeatedly that she was ignorant of current fashions.

Changing practices as well as the latest findings make dependence upon the standard text-book or reference books insufficient for the sole basis for the preparation of material. To safeguard against the inevitable dating of technical and commercial information the teacher should (1) read the journals of his trade and profession, (2) make use of subject abstracts and (3) keep an up-to-date filing system of references, articles and information of day-to-day reading, refresher courses and conversations.

When he has collected his information, the teacher will usually find that he has amassed far more material than he could or should present to his students. His next step is to discard:

1 Material that is not relevant to the background, needs and experiences of his students. For example, in a course on wines to new trainees who will shortly be waiting in a ship's dining room, the teacher will have to pare down all the information he could present on the various types of glass, the different types of wine and the many ways of serving wines and spirits. He would at this stage teach only enough to prevent mistakes which could prove both costly and embarrassing.

2 Material which amounts to his "hobby-horse" and which he could argue is not strictly related to the course content but which is nevertheless important to the clear understanding of the subject.

The teacher should establish his priorities. He should ensure that his final notebook contains the basis and essentials of the course — an irreducible minimum which is clearly defined. Then he should include whatever "cladding" he anticipates that time will permit. It is always wise to have extra material to hand for (*a*) a highly responsive class and (*b*) a class that will require remedial treatment.

Allied to the selection of course material is planning to have:

1 Accommodation available at the appropriate times in the course, e.g. language or science laboratory, typing room, workshop.

2 Illustrative "hardware", e.g. projectors, recording machines, television set.

3 Illustrative "software", e.g. films, loops, slides, transparencies, tapes.

4 Ingredients, e.g. in Catering subjects it is important to consider the availability of seasonal produce.

PREPARATION OF LESSONS AND LECTURES

The lesson is concerned with presenting facts, skills, ideas and attitudes to students and helping students to assimilate them. It enlists the active participation of students; it aims to help them retain the main points presented. For the majority of courses and students in Further Education the lesson is the most valuable vehicle of instruction. The lecture sometimes has a place in courses leading to work of the type associated with a university degree, although it needs to be backed up with discussion periods, directed reading and tutorials. Some general differences between lessons and lectures are:

Lesson	*Lecture*
Sets out to teach (reveal)	Sets out to give or tell information
Teacher more interested in his students	Lecturer more interested in his subject
Interplay between teacher and students	Interplay only if question time follows lecture
Teacher revises, builds on the old, tests the new	Lecturer assumes the audience is interested and able to follow the subject and learn later if necessary

STRUCTURE OF THE LECTURE

For teachers who need to give a synoptic view of their subject or to present a paper on their surveys or investigations, the lecture technique may be the fastest and most economical method of presenting their

information. Some excellent advice will be found on marshalling
evidence and presenting it in L. S. Powell's book, *Communications and
Learning.*

When a class is large the lecture method is often more appropriate.
The following is the plan of a lecture given to a class of 35 following
an Advanced Chemical Technicians' course. The material is divided
into headings and subheadings in topical sequence. Questions are
invited at the end of the talk.

Subject and level: Advanced Chemical   *Class:* T4   *Time:* 60 minutes
                Technicians

No. of students: 35

Lecture objectives

1 To outline the properties ot gasolines, kerosines, diesel fuels and
lubricants
2 To show how the performance depends on their chemistry and
composition
3 To show how the performance is modified by the use of chemical
additives

LECTURE PLAN

Time	*Stages and main points*			*Aids*
5 min	**Beginning** Review of previous week –		to show position on crude distillation of gasolines, kerosines, diesel oils and lubricants	Chalkboard diagram
	Middle			
	1 *Gasolines:*	*Easy starting –*	volatility – distillation curve	
		Cleanliness –	chemical composition, oxidation stability	CB build-up
15 min		*Economy (mpg) –*	calorific value correct volatility (distribution efficiency)	
		Ignition –	chemistry and octane no, use of additives vapour lock, icing, corrosion inhibition ·	

LECTURE PLAN (*continued*)

Time	Stages and main points			Aids
	Middle			
5 min	1 *Kerosines:*	*Clean burning* –	desulphurization, aromatics. Chemical markers, odorants	
10 min	3 *Diesel fuels:*	*Ignition quality*	cetane No.	
		Additives –	dopes, rust-inhibitors, markers for Customs & Excise. Lubrication of injector cylinders – viscosity	
20 min	4 *Lubricants (I.C. engines):*	*Detergent* –		
		Dispersants	Bearing corrosion-inhibitors, pour-point depressants viscosity index improvers defoamers	
5 min	**End** 5 *Lubricants:*		now a science on their own. Show extent: gear lubricants steam turbine textiles rolling oils cutting oils	CB summary
	6 *Tribology:*		new science of lubrication and wear; the reduction of friction by lubrication of moving parts	

PLANNING THE LESSON

The lesson material can be likened to a piece of cloth which must be tailored to the needs of a particular group of students in terms of the time allowed and the aids available. Often a period of contact between students and teacher may last from one to three hours. The long lesson calls for the "slow bowling" of ideas and frequent change of activity and frequent recapitulation. The lesson sheet given below indicates guidelines in the planning of units of work. The allocations of time to the various lesson "parts" should be tentative. Much depends upon class reactions and assimilation. The lesson plan is essentially flexible.

	Date:	*Time:*

Subject and level: *Class:*

Textbooks: *Background:*   *No. of students:*

(Previous knowledge.)

Lesson objectives:

(A statement of what the student should know and be able to do at the end of the lesson)

LESSON PLAN

Time	Stages and main points	Aids
	Beginning	
	1 Revision 2 Specific aim 3 Link-up of lesson with an appropriate interest common to students	
	Middle	
	4 Division of work between teacher and students 5 What is to be learned 6 How it is to be taught and presented 7 What students are expected to contribute 8 Questions to the class 9 Organization of individual and practical work	Apparatus, use of chalkboard and other teaching aids
	End	
	10 Summary and confirmation of salient points 11 Look forward to next lesson	

Many lessons in Further Education include (1) demonstration by the teacher, (2) practice by the students, (3) supervision and guidance by the teacher. The example which follows illustrates a fairly long lesson and deals with a topic which is not too technically worded to be followed by teachers of other subjects.

LESSON PLAN

Subject: **Ladies' Hairdressing**   *Syllabus:* City and Guilds 2

Topic: The Basic Set

Class: First Year Full Time Students   *Number:* 8

Background: have completed five weeks of course

Duration of Lesson: 1 hour 20 minutes

Time	Stages and main points	Aids
↑ 15 min ↓	**Introduction** *Aim:* to show that Hairdressing is not merely the placing of rollers and pin-curls in hair. Hairdressing is a fashion trade and so one employed in this trade must present a fashionable image to clients. *Appearance* is of utmost importance – a slovenly appearance can depict a person slovenly in all she does, a smart appearance conveys confidence. *Overalls* worn by male or female should be clean at all times. If overalls have ½ or ¾ sleeves, the sleeves of other garments should not show beneath those of the overall. Buttons on overalls should be fastened. Males should ensure that their collars are fastened and that ties are worn. *Stance* when attending client: demonstrate: (i) feet slightly apart (ii) left foot in front of right and alternating as movement made around client – thus distributing weight of body evenly (iii) shoulders back and head erect, rather like a "Cha-Cha" sequence. *Hygiene:* tools and implements should *not* be kept in pockets. Combs, scissors and razors should be arranged neatly on dressing table, together with a dish of antiseptic or disinfectant. Pockets collect fluff and breed germs. A common fault during "setting" is for clips or pins to be held in the hairdresser's mouth and then inserted in the client's hair. "Spitting" on client's hair must be avoided. *Safety:* dangerous to keep scissors or razors either in pockets or attached to buttons on front of overalls. Serious accidents may occur if the operator falls. *Incentive:* skill in hairdressing is simply the ability to control hair. Students' whole effort should be to master hair – to control hair, not to be controlled by hair.	 Draw attention to students offending these rules. Visual Aid No. 1 – Table layout Visual Aids No. 2 – Female hairdresser with tools in pockets, clips in mouth and attached to overall.

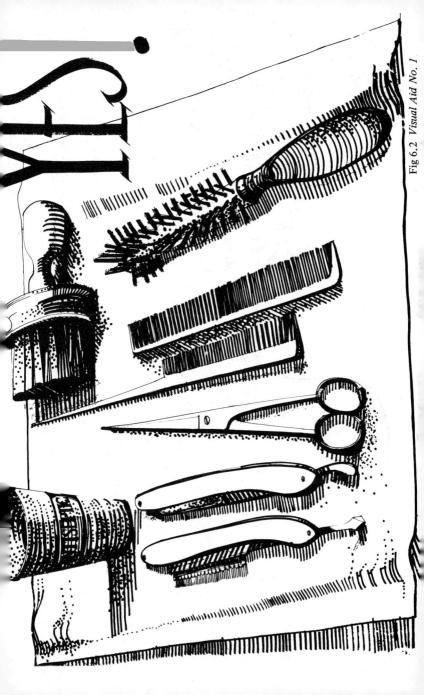

Fig 6.2 *Visual Aid No. 1*

Fig 6.3 *Visual Aid No. 2*

Time	Stages and main points	Aids
	Development: basic exercise in hair control.	
	Organization: models to be seated at dressing-tables. Models' hair previously shampooed. Students to be dealt with in two groups, four in each group. Group of four students will stand along-side so as to view demonstrator's actions from angle of operation.	
	Demonstration "A"	
	Correct method of combing hair after shampoo:	
10 min	1 Comb from the points of the hair, placing the free hand (left hand for right-handed person) on the head, lifting the hair slightly, ensuring comfort to client.	
	2 Work gradually from points of hair to frontal region.	
	3 Keep comb flat to the head.	
	Method of making a parting:	
	1 Use comb as marker.	
	2 Comb hair back from client's face, with comb held flat.	
	3 Outline a straight parting with comb.	
10 min	Key point: Advise students to ask "Madam" to slide down in chair, if working level is difficult.	
	Supervision: Circulate and give individual attention to each student.	
	Demonstration "B"	
	Key point: the sectioning of hair for placing of rollers should be oblong; the mesh of hair must not exceed in width the length of the roller.	
	1 Take section of hair and hold firmly at 45° from the head.	
	2 Place roller at the points of the hair.	
	3 Using thumbs of both hands as "needles" wind firmly down to the root section of hair.	
10 min	Comment: (1) holding the hair at 45° ensures maximum lift at the root. (2) In setting we endeavour to emulate natural movement in hair, which always stems from the root end of hair and not from the points. (3) Correct angle ensures that first two inches or so from the root end are not straight after the hair has been dried.	Visual Aid No. 3 – Correct and incorrect angle of rollers.
	Demonstration speed: first normal – then slower than normal – finally back to normal.	
10 min	*Practice:* check points: (1) Stance, (2) Students' comfort, (3) Size of sections of hair in relation to size of rollers – correct size of section of hair.	

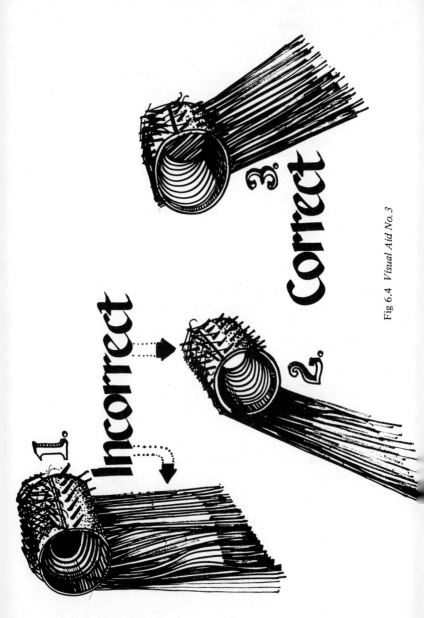

Incorrect

1.

2.

3. **Correct**

Fig 6.4 *Visual Aid No. 3*

Time	Stages and main points	Aids
↑ I 10 min | ↓	*Demonstration "C"* Explanation: the pin-curl is an attempt to emulate naturally curly hair, hair that curls from the root and not from the points of the hair. Key points: (1) take a square section of hair. (2) Place the index finger of the left hand at the root and shape. (3) Form a circle at the points and wind up. (4) Finally reshape at the root and place the circle of hair to fit snugly and fix with a clip. Demonstration sequence: normal speed —,then slower — finally back to normal.	Visual Aid No. 4 — Steps in producing pin-curl
↑ I 10 min | ↓	*Practice:* check points: 1 Commonplace bad practice of wrapping hair around finger to form circle for pin-curls, so leaving straight hair at the root end. 2 Working stance. 3 Combs should not have teeth missing. 4 Metal clips should not be touching model's face, as heat from dryer could cause burns.	
↑ I 3 min | ↓	*Demonstration "D"* Application of net and ear shields. Explanation: the hair net is put on client's hair on completion of set, to safeguard the rollers and clips from loosening, as air circulates in dryer. The ear shields protect the ears of the model from the hot air of the dryer.	
↑ 2 min ↓	**Conclusion** Models are scrutinized. Students check nets and ear shields and escort models from salon.	

FURTHER READING

H L Hill "Lesson Preparation", *The Technical Journal* December 1966 (pages 9–12)

L S Powell *Communication and Learning,* Chapter 4 (pages 47–62) Pitman 1969

Square Section of Hair.

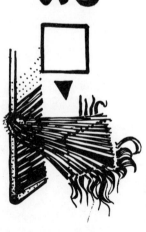

Shaping at the root.

Form clean circle and wind tightly up.

Fig 6.5 Visual Aid No. 4

7

Presentation (1)

The written and the spoken word remains the chief means of putting across ideas and information. Teaching is communication: the teacher's conveying information, skills, attitudes and ideas; the student's receiving these, understanding them, appreciating them, and storing them. One of the teacher's most frequently recurring functions is to present his material in language — spoken or written — which is readily understood by those who have to *act* upon it. In order to convey his subject, he must take account of the feelings and spirit of his students. The true measure of teaching is the whole effect it has on the students. Before a teacher can start putting his stuff across, he must make some sort of contact with his students. Ideally he should pitch his teaching at an appropriate level of difficulty, so that the student's anxiety is at an optimum, neither too high nor too low.

ORAL PRESENTATION

Some American teachers deliberately spend the first ten minutes of any teaching period establishing at least contact and preferably concord with a class. No significant technical information is conveyed; the emphasis is on non-technical information. The teacher is feeling his way towards a starting point. An introductory warming-up period, consisting of rather meaningless exchanges of words with students can often be effective in paving the way for students to attend and receive whatever message the teacher intends to present. These preliminaries to a lesson, whether or not they are designed, can establish a bond or "phatic communion" with students.

ATTENTION

The teacher who wishes to hold his students' attention should consider three questions:

1 For how long can students listen?
2 How much material should be presented?
3 What are the vocabulary and verbal reasoning powers of the learners?

For short periods of time the mind can take in ideas at an extremely high rate, so continuous talking should usually be limited to ten minutes. It is wiser to introduce "strainbreakers", if the aim is to present a closely reasoned argument. "Strainbreakers" could take the form of pauses, visual illustration or a story which acts as an example.

For research purposes the talk on "A Metric System" below was given by the author to a variety of classes in a College of Further Education. It was spoken more or less from memory so as to establish as much eye-contact as possible with the students. A large number of points were made in a short time. The style is very matter-of-fact and impersonal, the style of a report. Students in the 15—19 age group found the content of no great interest. With a technical topic in which new material is being presented orally, continuous exposition for as long as ten minutes could be disastrous for the listening comprehension of many young workers.

A METRIC SYSTEM

There can be no doubt that the decimal system is unsurpassed in simplicity and convenience; on every practical ground it is far superior to the present law of the jungle prevailing in British currency and measurements. The basic units of the metric system of weights and measures (the metre and kilogramme) may in themselves be no better than the yard and the pound; the great advantage of the metric system throughout is an application of the decimal system. It is, indeed, the decimal system in action, its multiples and fractions being in terms of tens, hundreds, or thousands of the basic units.

How well suited this system is to our civilization becomes clear when we consider that our ordinary numeral system itself is, for better or worse, the decimal system. Just as, in the rising scales of the metric system, each higher unit is ten times the amount of the nearer lower one, so in the ordinary numeral system the progressive shift of the individual digits from right to left indicates a tenfold increase. Any multiplication sum in the metric system can thus be completed by a simple use of the decimal point. For instance, 5 × 25 centimetres is 1·25 metres, or one metre, two decimetres, five centimetres. Compare this with multiplying 25 inches by 5, giving three yards, one foot, five inches, or think of turning gallons into cubic feet, with the relations between units differing in each case, and the term "law of the jungle" for the rules of British measurements may not seem unjustified.

A serious drawback of the non-metric system in Great Britain is that large parts of the world use the decimal system. Obviously a British manufacturer who exports to a decimal-system country has to incur a lot of extra trouble and cost in order to deliver his goods in the specifications of the purchasing country. Yet in 1952 the British Government rejected the Hodges Report of 1951, which advocated the adoption of the metric system here. What are the reasons for this negative attitude?

We have to reckon, first, with a sentimental attachment to old, familiar ways and a certain dislike of a coldly scientific terminology. But this kind of sentiment is surely passing. New fields of knowledge and activity in science and technology are already dominated by the decimal system: few who have to deal with them find anything strange in kilowatts and milligrammes.

A more valid reason is that in some parts of the world very important for us (the Commonwealth countries and the USA) the metric system is only partially, or even not at all, in use, although this objection applies much less to currency, for the dollar is based on the decimal system, and many parts of the Commonwealth have followed the States here. So now has India, in spite of great difficulties.

For measurements, the problem is much less simple. It is to a large extent a question of deciding with which part of the world we intend to conform more closely. One point we have to consider in making our choice is the likelihood that the underdeveloped countries, with which we can expect to do a great deal of trade, will tend to accept the decimal system because of its association with modern science and technology, on which their progress largely depends.

There is no denying that in the realm of measurements the industrial change-over, especially in such branches as precision engineering, would face difficulties which may seem prohibitive, although there are few technical problems nowadays which cannot be solved, given unlimited funds, and the Hodges Committee, in fact, suggested that the change could be completed in twenty years. But let us grant that the task is formidable and forbidding when viewed as a whole. What is certainly possible is a gradual advance towards the goal, with the change made first in particularly suitable fields. In this way the gradual acceptance of a complete metric system in this country will in the long run surely come about. Time — and time-saving — are both on its side.

In his letter to the Corinthians St Paul makes a memorable observation: "If with your tongue, you fail to utter intelligible words, how will people know what you are saying? You will be talking to the air".[1] The teacher of every subject is faced with the problems of vocabulary

[1] I Corinthians xiv 9

— "Will they get this?" "What is their background for understanding that?" and "If we put this word in for the brightest ones, will it hold up the weaker brethren?" Rudolf Flesch has a useful formula for producing "plain talk" and predicting its intelligibility for particular groups. He suggests that a plain, easy-to-follow style of exposition results from:

1 Short sentences.
2 Few affixes, i.e. word appendages such as *pro-* in progressive, and *-ology* in terminology.
3 Plenty of personal references, i.e. references to people, either by name or by the use of personal pronouns, such as "you", "I" and "they"

By Flesch's criteria the talk on "A Metric System" can be analysed as follows:

Average sentence	Number of affixes per 100 words	Number of personal references per 100 words	Description of style
26 words	46	2	Difficult

RECEPTION

Students tended to lose interest in this talk, which gives some support to Flesch's idea that long sentences, many long words and few personal references make for listening fatigue. This is particularly true of students who have no previous background of training in listening. Nevertheless an investigation of how much students had learned from this talk revealed that some subject matter which was beyond them in print became intelligible to them when the work of interpretation was done for them by the teacher, through his emphases and variation in pace, pitch and tone. This is the main justification for oral presentation.

NON-VERBAL COMMUNICATION

In the playback of a recorded talk, the importance of tones of voice is apparent; what are lacking are the powerful factors of looks and gestures. The teacher shows that he *wishes* to present information to his students by looking at them, by making *eye-contact*. From eye-contact the teacher judges whether he is getting his points over, and whether the student is confused or wishes to ask a question.

The most obvious way to reinforce the spoken word is with the pointed forefinger, shaking it, raising it, jabbing it. Finer shades can be expressed by pressing thumb and forefinger together. Two-handed poses can help with the balancing of the pros and cons of a subject. The clenched fist can portray conviction; and the destructive sweep with both palms can convey a sense of urgency. The essence of gesture is that it should concentrate, not dissipate, students' attention.

Clothes can facilitate or impede communication. The teacher should consider whether his dress gives him confidence in himself is suitable to his position or the subject he is teaching, and whether it gives students confidence in him.

USE OF THE VOICE

The teacher should be audible, if he wishes students to "tune in" to his talk. Too few take the precaution of checking if they can be heard by all students in a group. The following are elementary measures which help to overcome the most frequent barriers to communication:

1 Speak up but do not shout; hoarseness at the end of a lesson results from the faulty use of the voice.
2 Put sufficient power into the speaking of words at the end of a sentence to make them easily heard.
3 Form consonants crisply at the end of words.
4 Avoid blurring one word with another.
5 Vary the pitch of the voice: a high pitch is easier to hear but a low pitch more pleasant to listen to.
6 Be clear and precise without being aggressive.
7 Emphasize key words and subordinate unimportant words — this gives a significant rhythm to speech.
8 Co-ordinate posture, facial expression and gesture with tone of voice to give listeners an impression of sincerity, confidence and friendliness.
9 Pronounce words so as to cause neither ambiguity nor embarassment to listeners.

INSTRUCTIONS, ORAL AND WRITTEN

Instructions are spoken during or at the end of demonstrations in laboratory and workroom, before the students begin their period of practice. It happens frequently that instructions are given only once, and disconnectedly, during a demonstration, with the final step of the instruction given immediately before the students start to practise. Almost invariably the final operation is remembered better than the first, and the middle items least well. Spoken instructions are followed better if they are (*a*) repeated, (*b*) supported by written instructions.

The following is a transcript of instructions spoken to building apprentices before they were to carry out a "Slump Test".

THE SLUMP TEST

When batching concrete the correct proportions of cement, sand, and coarse aggregate must be maintained throughout the job, so that allowance must be made for the "bulking" of the sand. The standard test for bulking is based on the fact that while damp sand bulks, the volume of saturated sand — completely soaked with water — is the same as if the sand were dry.

To make the test, you will need any straight-sided container — a 2 lb jam-jar, for instance, or a clean, empty can, and a rule, a steel rod to rod the sand with, a second container to tip it into, and some water.

First fill the container about two-thirds full with the sand you are testing. Drop it in loosely; do not pack it down. Level off the top, and, pushing a steel rule through it to the bottom, measure the height of the sand. Suppose this is 6 inches.

Now that you know the height of the damp, bulked sand, your next step is to find the height of the same sand when saturated with water. You can then compare the two. Empty the sand into another container (taking care that none of it is lost in the process) and half fill the first container with water. You are now going to put the sand back into the water, bit by bit, so that it is entirely saturated. First put back about half the sand and rod it thoroughly to remove any air. Then add the rest and rod again in the same way and level off the top. Now push your rule through the sand as before and measure the new height. You find that it has sunk noticeably.

Assume that the sand now measures 5 inches. You know that this sand, which when saturated (or dry) measures 5 inches, bulks to 6 inches when damp. The bulking on 5 inches of dry sand is thus 1 inch. From this you can calculate the percentage bulking, in this case 20 per cent. The volume of sand used should therefore be 20 per cent more than quoted in the specification. If you are batching by weight no adjustment is necessary as the weight hardly alters.

The subsequent performance of the students suggested that they understood the content of the three-minute talk. The words are easy, the sentences are mostly short, and the student is addressed personally as "you". However, a number of them found that they had forgotten the sequence of operations. This may be attributed to the teacher's giving too much instruction or information before the students attempted their task. Translating words into action may easily exceed the capacity of the learner.

Some general advice upon the phrasing of instructions would be:

1 Avoid sentences which begin "Don't —" or "No —", particularly when the information is new.
2 Prefer the simple declarative sentence, e.g. "Remove tacks and turn sleeve to wrong side", to the less easily understood form: "Tacks should be removed and sleeve turned to the wrong side".

SEQUENTIAL OPERATIONS

The teacher should make a rigorous analysis of a task, before he can tell students exactly what they should do. To give instructions for the performance of sequential operations, he should break these up into manageable units. Fig 7.1 shows an extract from a diagram giving a step-by-step sequence of operations for a marking-out exercise for apprentices in the iron and steel industry. They have been given the drawing of the job and this diagram provides the procedural steps so that the students can approach the job in an orderly and confident manner.

Fig 7.1 *A step-by-step sequence of operations for a marking-out exercise*

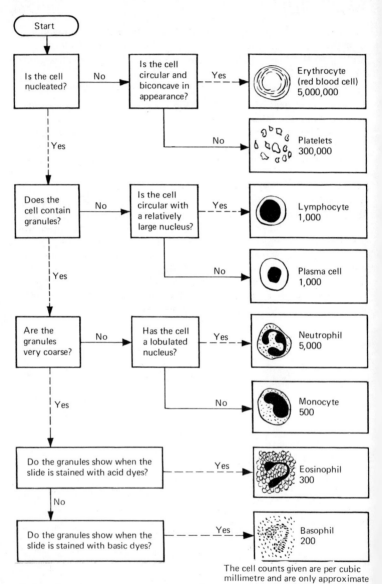

Fig 7.2 *Identification of blood cells seen on a blood smear under a microscope*

THE LOGICAL TREE METHOD

The conventional presentation of instructions and rules in prose can be a long-winded and ineffective method of communicating certain procedural and diagnostic skills. It is not possible, for example, to give brief and effective instructions on how to identify eight different kinds of blood cells from observation of a blood smear under a microscope, until the teacher has done an error factor analysis of possible misunderstandings. The "logical tree" method guides the student by a series of simple questions each of which can be answered by "yes" or "no".

This example is a particular type of "algorithm" or recipe for solving a problem, or conveying information, particularly of complex and inter-related rules. This method has the merit of showing students exactly what information they need and of excluding anything that is irrelevant. (See Fig. 7.2.)

FURTHER READING

B N Lewis and R J Woolfenden *Algorithms and Logical Trees: A Self Instructional Course,* 1969, Cambridge Algorithms Press

R Flesch *The Art of Plain Talk,* 1949, New York, Harper

F E Foden *Efficient English for Technical Students,* 1964 (Chapter 14 pages 164–9), University of London Press

8

Presentation (2)

STUDENTS' NOTES

The storage of information is the final stage in the teaching process.
Note-taking is necessary to almost every subject. "A good set of notes"
according to student folklore is important for examination success.
The kinds of notes to be found in a student's file will reflect (*a*) the
success with which a teacher puts his material over and (*b*) the
amount of guidance he has given in making notes.

DICTATION

To make a regular habit of dictating notes continuously for more
than a couple of minutes can scarcely be termed teaching. Nothing
blunts the students' minds, which should be active and curious, more
than a dictation lesson. Dictation is, however, justified when the
precise wording of a note is vital, for instance, where some important
"law" or statement has to be taken down. If it is not in the textbook
used by the student, he may wish the teacher to formulate the
statement in the precise terms in which it should be remembered.

COPYING FROM CHALKBOARD

Another practice is for the teacher to write full notes on the chalkboard to be copied into the student's notebook. An example is given
here:

HINTS ON DRILLING

1 Keep drills sharp. Do not wait until they are "dull" before re-
sharpening. Forcing a dull drill is bad economy, for when it does
give out, considerably more will have to be ground off than otherwise would have been the case.
2 Use recommended lubricants. Take care to ensure that the lubri-
cant reaches the point of the drill.
3 Do not allow the drill flutes to become choked with drillings.
4 The work must be held rigid and the drill spindle should have no
end play.
5 When the drill is re-ground, see that the correct point angles are
produced.

6 Use multi-fluted drills for opening out existing or cored holes. Two fluted drills are not designed for this purpose.
7 When driving the drill into its socket use a hammer made of some soft material. Make certain that there is a good fit between the taper shank of the drill and the sleeve or socket, otherwise the tang may break.
8 The chuck in which the straight shank drill is held must be of good quality. If the drill slips in the chuck and the feed is automatic, breakage of the drill is inevitable.

DRILLING LUBRICANTS (RECOMMENDED)	
Hard tool and alloy steel	Soda water or soluble oil compound
Mild steel	Good cutting compound soluble oil
Copper Brass Some bronzes	Dry or paraffin
Bronzes which cause heating up	Soluble oil
Aluminium Magnesium alloy	Paraffin. Soluble oil
Cast Iron	Work dry. If possible cool drill with jet of compressed air.
Stainless steels Nimonics	Soluble oil sometimes satisfactory, but sulphurized and chlorinated mineral or fatty oils may improve finish and prolong drill life.
Perspex	Soluble oil will improve finish.

A cursory glance at the students' notebook after the copying session revealed that many students are not accurate in their transcriptions. The provision and circulation of ready-made duplicated notes is preferable to this; indeed, sometimes essential with classes of students who are not capable of taking their own notes or of learning to take them, let alone making their own notes.

NOTE-TAKING
Few students can boast a memory so retentive as to be able to eschew note-taking. As the Chinese proverb has it, "The faintest ink is better than the most retentive memory". The requirement of note-taking encourages attention to the lesson, makes the student think and should train him in the skill of selection.

It is of the first importance that the teacher should give guidance in making notes. He can signpost the important points of a lesson and note them on the chalkboard (or some suitable substitute such as the overhead projector). He should give a sufficient lead to ensure that the student is able to note:

1 The main points.
2 References.
3 Definitions, important data.

The student should take notes in sufficient detail to illustrate the main points and to preserve an element of continuity. Students tend to produce inadequate notes because of:

1 Lack of familiarity with the material.
2 Inability to realize when something significant has been said.
3 Inability to concentrate.
4 Distractions by their fellow students.
5 The turgid content of the lesson, which dispels interest.

Structured note-taking

A useful method is to distribute a sheet with the main headings and key points with spaces to be filled in as the lesson progresses. This also applies to diagrams to be labelled and maps to be completed. Note-taking of a general studies lesson on "The Channel Crossing" might be structured as follows:

THE CHANNEL CROSSING

1   The purpose of a continuous crossing is to:

      Convey (*a*) ....
      Convey (*b*) ....

      Speed up ....

      Ease Trade

2   Forms of transport using crossing:

      (*a*)

      (*b*)

3   Threefold choice:

      (*a*) .... Tunnel

      (*b*) .... Tunnel

      (*c*) Bridge

4 Theoretical considerations are not the most important things about struc-
tures. The most important things are ....
....

5 *Bored Tunnel* Two types (*a*) .... (*b*) ....
Chalk is one of the best materials for tunnelling because ....
....

6 The length would be about ....

7 *Immersed Tunnels* are constructed by...
easier to operate because ventilation is not so difficult and to construct
because ....
The main difficulty in the English Channel would be ....
.... and wrecks.

8 *Bridge* is possible — Lake Pontchartrain 22 miles long — the main difference
in the problem is the amount of ....

9 *Cost, etc.*

		Cost	Time to Build	Yield
Bored Tunnel	Rail —	£..		
	Road —	£..		
	Mixed —	£..		
Immersed Tunnel	Road —	£..		
	Rail —	£..		
	Mixed —	£..		
Bridge	Mixed —	£..		

QUESTIONING

It is the responsibility of teachers to ensure that their students have
absorbed their instructions in exactly the way that they, the teachers,
have intended that it should be understood. It is also the teacher's
business to find out what the students already know so that the lesson
can proceed from that which they do know to that which they do

not. And it is their further business, whenever possible, to make students establish *for themselves* the knowledge they seek to teach, and the students, presumably, wish to acquire.

Socrates being asked "What is justice?" does not give a direct answer; he puts questions to his questioner and others, and gets them to clear their own ideas, and finally a great treatise on the principles of government emerges as the complete and elaborate answer to the original question. This "Socratic" method of teaching, pursued intelligently and without waste of time, is perhaps the most effective of all teaching methods: for it enlists completely the minds of the students, who attain knowledge by their *own direct efforts*.

You become a skilled questioner by questioning, but the following observations may help the inexperienced teacher.

1   Questions should always be explicit and unambiguous. The student should have no excuse for not understanding what he or she is being asked. Some examples of what should be avoided may be helpful:
(a) Do you know what is involved in *job analysis*?
    A correct answer would be "yes" or "no", which is certainly *not* the object of the question. A better form of the question is: What is involved in job analysis?
(b) Is starboard denoted by red or green? In preference ask: What colour denotes starboard?
(c) Sandra, is it branching or linear? (The reply may be: What do branching and linear mean?)
And, lastly, an example which should be unique but is not:
(d) "Now, of course, we want *your* opinion of river pollution and you are free to say what you like, even if you haven't thought about it very much, for it's difficult, isn't it, and we all have our opinions but putting on one side our prejudices, generally don't you think? — that is to say —. What I mean to say is —." And so it goes droning on.
The first important principle therefore is, let your question be a question and *nothing more*. And let it be brief, direct, and as a rule admit of one answer only. Here it is advisable to employ the H and W rule, that is, begin each question with How or What, When, Who, Which? Do not give the student a chance to guess.

2   Leading questions, that is to say, questions which suggest the answer, are in teaching not necessarily to be avoided. But they should be used sparingly. Much depends upon the purpose of the question. If its purpose is to *establish* knowledge, then the question itself may well suggest the answer.

If the teacher's aim is to examine students to see whether certain knowledge has been acquired or whether a process of reasoning has been followed, a leading question is inappropriate.
Direct questions should be used:

What are machine tools and how do they work?
Who uses them and why are they vital to our industrial progress?
Who makes them and how has the British industry developed?
How does Britain stand in selling machine tools to export markets?
What are the developments in new techniques and in automation?

3 It is better to avoid elliptical questions, i.e. the question put in the form that merely requires a missing word to be inserted, usually at the end, e.g. Is a sample a portion of a —? (population)

It is pedantic and unnecessary to prescribe that an answer must be in a complete sentence. A sentence need be used only where necessary. This is often required in language teaching when the main object is to practise students in constructing sentences:

Q. La capitale de la France est . . .?
A. Paris est la capitale de la France.
Q. La capitale de la Grande Bretagne est . . .?
A. Londres est la capitale de la Grande Bretagne.

In other cases the monosyllabic reply is often justified. If the teacher asks "Do you agree with this?" the ordinary answer is "Yes" or "No". This should be accepted even if it should be followed by the further question "Why?" or "Why not?"

4 Courtesy is desirable in questioning a class of adolescents or adults. They feel the presence of their fellows. Accept answers and make the best, not the worst, of them. It will often be necessary to show that they are wrong or inadequate, but see that this is done quietly, straight-forwardly, kindly. Listen hard and help the student to express himself:

Listen to what he wants to say;
to what he doesn't want to say;
and to what he can't say without your help.

Questioning gives students a channel not only for expressing technical or "operating" data, but also for expressing their underlying attitudes, fears and hopes. A little praise for a *thoughtful* answer even if it is incorrect is invariably profitable.

5 Another important principle is concerned with the urge that many teachers have to continue questioning beyond the point at which it is possible. They often tend to go on attempting to "elicit" information or ideas that the students are plainly unable to supply. If the class does not know the answer to the question asked, *tell them* or let them, for example, find out by reading.

6 Questions should be distributed evenly over the whole class. This rarely occurs. Make a point of questioning each member of a class in any lesson, whenever the size of the class permits. Too frequently teachers have a "preferred side" on which to pose questions.

7 The occasions on which questions are used are as important as their form. We may conceive of an oral lesson as having a number of sections, each section having a series of paragraphs, each containing a point. As we conclude the development of each section and each paragraph we should ask a few brief questions to see whether the point has been appreciated. Recapitulation at the end of a lesson is often most effectively done by way of question and answer.

8 Not infrequently a later lesson in a series may well open with a few questions on the last one given. This serves to refresh the memory, and to establish continuity with what has gone before.

9 It is difficult to determine how far questions by the class should be permitted and encouraged. A genuine question should *never* be met with a snub. An irrelevant question should be declared irrelevant. It is often expedient to permit questions by students during the currency of an expository lesson, provided they are not allowed to interrupt the lesson to the degree that brings about waste of time.

THE QUIZ

A battery of questions may be used to revise and consolidate information. The quiz which follows revises a lesson given some weeks previously on Floors and Floor Finishes and prepares for a demonstration on large-scale cleaning equipment for floors.

QUIZ ON FLOORS AND FLOORING

1 *Q.* What are the main points to be considered when buying floorings?
  A. Any three: durability, suitability, cost (intitial and maintenance), comfort, sound and heat insulation, appearance.

2 *Q.* What is a sub-floor?
  A. The surface under a floor or floor-finish.

3 *Q.* From what may sub-floors be made?
  A. Wood or concrete.

4 *Q.* What are the main drawbacks to both these types of sub-floor?
  A. Rising damp and dry rot.

5 *Q.* Name some of the types of floor finishes available?
  A. Granolithic, bitumastic, tiled, wood, semi-hard.

6 *Q*. What is a granolithic floor finish?
  A. Granite chips set in cement.

7 *Q*. What is the difference between granolithic and terrazzo?
  A. Terrazzo is a mixture of marble and other chips set in cement.

8 *Q*. Where would these two finishes be used?
  A. Foyers, cloakrooms, kitchens.

9 *Q*. Where would you use a magnesite floor? and why?
  A. Linen-room or anywhere where there is little likelihood of much water being spilt. Magnesite is very porous so washing is to be avoided.

10 *Q*. What is a bitumastic floor?
   A. A type of asphalt rolled onto a solid sub-floor in a hot plastic state.

11 *Q*. What are the uses of this flooring?
   A. Bathrooms and to prevent rising damp in other floor finishes.

12 *Q*. What is the difference between quarry and ceramic tiles?
   A. Quarry are fired to make them harder and so are less absorbent (but more slippery). Ceramic are glazed and used for more decorative purposes; have wider colour range.

13 *Q*. State the uses of quarry and ceramic tiling?
   A. Quarry – cloakrooms, kitchens, canteens, food preparation.
     Ceramic – bathrooms, decorations.

14 *Q*. What is the difference between block and parquet wood flooring?
   A. Block floors are laid on an adhesive on a level concrete base.
     Parquet floors are made from thinner wood and are pinned and glued to a wooden sub-floor.

15 *Q*. Describe a strip wood floor.
   A. Lengths of narrow strips (under 4 inches wide) from hardwood of good appearance. These are fixed to joists or timber insets in concrete. (A sprung floor has springs under the joists to increase resilience.)

16 *Q*. Where would you use block, strip and parquet floors?
   A. Linen-rooms, storerooms, staff halls. Ballrooms. Foyers and lounges.

17 *Q*. What are thermoplastic floorings?
   A. They are made from a variety of asphaltic materials and are put down in a warm state. They harden on cooling.

18 *Q*. Uses for vinyl tiled floors?
   A. Bathrooms, cloakrooms, canteens, corridors, offices.

19 *Q*. Uses of rubber flooring?
   A. Bathrooms and under non-slip mats, also bars.

20 *Q*. What are the different types of linoleum?
   A. Inlaid and printed pattern.

21 *Q*. What are the advantages of cork tiles?
   A. Quiet and warm, can be sealed.

22 *Q*. What is the point of using a floor seal?
   A. A seal gives a non-absorbent semi-permanent finish. Minimizes labour.

23 *Q.* What precautions should be taken to prevent accidents on all floor finishes?
  A. Fasten loose edges. Use metal strips on edges of floorings near doorways to prevent edges sticking up. Avoid excessive water when cleaning.

24 *Q.* What is the daily cleaning routine for floorings?
  A. Remove dust and dirt by sweeping, vacuum-cleaning, mopping or washing according to type of flooring.

QUESTIONS AND NOTES FOR A LESSON

The lesson in welding science, which follows, illustrates a plan based upon questions, which are posed at each stage of the lesson, and upon chalkboard notes, which are to be copied by the students. Chalkboard diagrams are also to be copied. There is always a danger of students spending too long on copying chalkboard work. A time limit is essential to avoid the loss of too much class time.

Course: Welding Science   **Topic:** Crystal Structures

Aim: To reinforce the previous week's lecture and demonstration on the various crystal structures in a cast ingot or weld, plus the defects in cast or welded structures.

Introductory Questions
  1 From what type of metal do metallic crystals form?
  2 How do they form and what is the name given to the shape?

Aid
  Diagram
  3 How would you sketch it?
  4 What governs its size?
  5 What type of crystalline structure would we see if we sectioned the ingot?
  6 Why would we see varying shapes?

Lesson
Instructions relative to the notes.

Aid
Sketch of sectioned ingot to be copied at end of notes.

Question
  7 What defects would you expect to find in a cast structure?

Chalkboard Notes
Defects in Cast Structures
Blow-holes: These are caused by furnace gases which have dissolved in the metal during melting or by chemical reactions, and upon cooling are thrown out of solution. Some dendrite arms having already formed trap the gas and it appears as irregular shapes occurring at almost any point in the structure.

Questions

8 What causes shrinkage?
9 What other name is given to it?
10 How can you prevent piping occurring during welding and casting?

Aid

Sketch of ingot showing piping to be copied at end of notes
Models

Chalkboard Notes

Shrinkage: When a metal solidifies its volume decreases and because this shrinkage occurs the mould must be designed that there is always a header of molten metal called a riser which solidifies last. Shrinkage is also responsible for the effect known as piping, which is usually found in the area of molten metal that freezes last.

Questions

11 What types of impurities are likely to be found in cast structures?
12 What happens to these impurities?

Chalkboard Notes

Segregation of Impurities

(a) The dendrites which form first are of almost pure metal, thus impurities become progressively more concentrated in the liquid that remains. Hence the metal which freezes last at the grain boundaries contains the bulk of impurities. This is known as Minor Segregation.

Aid

Sketch of Minor Segregation to be copied.

Question

13 What happens to the impurities still in the molten metal?

Chalkboard Notes

(b) As the columnar crystals grow inwards they push some of the impurities in front of them. In this way much of the impurities become concentrated in the central pipe. This is known as Major Segregation.

Aid

Sketch of Major Segregation to be copied.

Chalkboard Notes

(c) Major or Inverse V segregation is caused by the impure metal just in front of the columnar crystals (having a lower melting point) freezing last. The metal at the centre begins to form large equi-axed crystals so that the impure molten metal is trapped in an intermediate position. This is indicated by a V-shape marking in a etched section.

Summary of main points followed by *questions.*

FURTHER READING

H R Mills *Teaching and Training,* 1967 (pages 66–72), Macmillan

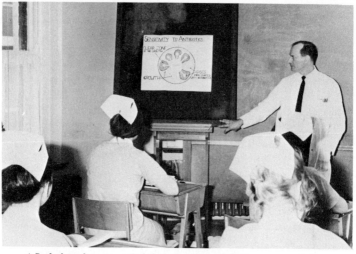

A Pathology lecture to Ophthalmic Nurses showing a prepared chart on a magnetic board

A group investigation: a group of motor vehicle students under supervision in a Technical College workshop (Photo: S Chandra)

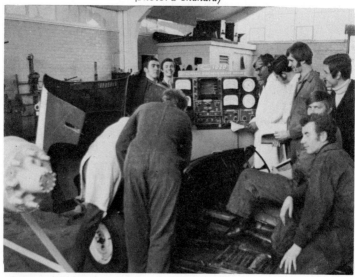

Demonstration of paint removal to a group of craft apprentices in a Painting and Decorating class

Adults attending a class on Decimal Currency (Photo: S Chandra)

9

Subject and Method

It is the nature of the subject which determines the teaching method. Therefore, before beginning to teach, think carefully over the general object to be achieved by the study of the subject taught. Thus, for example, the object of teaching or learning shorthand is that the student shall acquire the power of taking down rapidly, accurately, and in an intelligible script the *spoken* word. Many of the subjects taught in Further Education will require practical classes, where the teacher's demonstration is followed by the students' supervised practice. Most lessons will involve methods which will be a variation of "tell and quiz". Often the best way to teach is to incorporate several techniques in one lesson.

LABORATORY WORK

Well conceived laboratory work would seek to develop observational skills, selective ability, classificatory skill and discrimination.

In certain science courses approximately one-third of the total teaching time is spent in the laboratory. There must be no time wasted by the students and therefore preparation for laboratory work is as vital as is classroom lesson preparation. The issue of a handout, which gives clear statement of the laboratory exercise, materials and equipment, procedure and finally some indication of conclusions, makes for efficient use of time and resources. The following handout or laboratory sheet served this purpose:

DIVERSITY IN CELL STRUCTURE

Purpose

This is an observational exercise in which the structure of a number of different kinds of living cells are compared.

Materials and Equipment

Microscope	Gram's Iodine
Forceps, fine	Methylene blue
Dissecting needles	Ringer's solution
Scalpel	Paper towels
Scissors	Onion
Slides, plain	Elodea leaves
Cover-slips	Frog skin
Droppers	Frog muscle

Procedure

A. Epidermal Cells of Onion

1 Peel off the inner skin (epidermis), trim and place on slide.
2 Add 1 drop of water and cover slip.
3 Examine under low power.
4 Draw a section of the field to show the arrangement of the cells.
5 Irrigate with Gram's Iodine.
6 Note any changes.
7 Change to high power and draw one cell. Label.

B. Cells of Elodea Leaf

1 Remove the tip from a young leaf and place on slide.
2 Add 1 drop of water and cover-slip.
3 Examine under low power.
4 Note the number of cell layers (adjust fine focus).
5 Change to high power and draw one cell. Label.

C. Cells of Human Cheek

1 Gently scrape the inside of the cheek with back of finger nail.
2 Transfer the smear to a clean slide.
3 Add 1 drop of methylene blue and cover-slip.
4 Centre under low power, change to high power and examine.
5 Draw one or two cells. Label.

D. Cells of Frog Skin

1 Place scrapings of frog skin on a clean slide.
2 Add 1 drop of Ringer's solution and cover-slip.
3 Centre under low power, change to high power and examine.
4 Draw one or two cells. Label.

E. Cells of Frog Muscle

1. Place a small piece of frog muscle on a slide. Add 1 drop of Ringer's solution and tease the sample apart using two needles.
2 Add 1 drop of methylene blue and cover-slip.
3 Examine under low power and locate thinnest part of material.
4 Change to high power and draw a small section. Label.

SUMMARY: On the basis of your observations can you form any conclusions about the differences between plant and animal cells?
Compare (*a*) cytoplasm, (*b*) cell wall, (*c*) nucleus of plant and animal cells.

DEMONSTRATION

To teach a skill or a process the demonstration method is frequently employed. The assumption is made that showing gives the student insight into what is involved in the task or jobs. He imitates what he has seen and practises the job under guidance until he acquires skill. It is frustrating for students to feel "as if their whole vocation were endless imitation", even though a solid foundation of basic skills should be laid before most students can extemporize or produce variations. The teacher should always make an effort to show the relevance of the skill to the students' progress. The teaching procedure will vary according to the type of skill and the number of students that may be effectively taught. However, the following steps are usually followed:

Before demonstrating:

1 Break down skill or job into units.
2 Analyse each stage and key point and formulate questions.
3 Position the group to see from the operator's point of view as far as possible.

Conducting the demonstration:

4 State the skill or subject.
5 Create interest in the skill.
6 Describe, show and illustrate the skill one stage at a time.
7 Stress key points.

Practice:

8 Arrange initial practice, if possible for an individual from the group.
9 Stop individual student where appropriate and invite group to confirm or correct his performance as necessary.
10 Summarize main points.
11 Supervise practice of each student.

A 20-minute demonstration of Silver Soldering illustrates some of these points.

Subject: Silver Soldering   *Class:* Electrical Technicians   *Time:* 20 mins

No. of students: 8

Lesson objectives:

To show how to join metal by silver soldering
To point out common errors
To test the joint for strength
To examine the joint visually

Equipment

1 Exercise ready for silver soldering -- silver solder – flux
2 Degreasant – Stillson wrench – hacksaw – chisel – hammer

LESSON PLAN

Time	Stages and main points
4 min	**Beginning** What silver soldering is The joining together of metal by heating to required temperature and applying flux and silver solder Why student should know how to silver solder Will need to join parts of his workpieces together at a later stage of the course
10 min	**Middle** *Preparing workpiece* 1 Remove scale from bar and ensure that it fits freely in the block. 2 Degrease and assemble. *Positioning workpiece* 1 Shielded by fire bricks in order to get maximum heat. 2 In subdued light. *Heating workpiece and applying flux* 1 Heat to a "black heat" and apply flux. *Heating workpiece and applying solder* 1 Heat to dull red and apply solder. *Caution:* Do not overheat; will burn flux and prevent it doing its job. *Testing workpiece for strength* Grip in vice and test with "stillson wrench". Twist until bar turns a little. *Examining workpiece* 1 Saw down centre of block. 2 "Splay" out with chisel. 3 Examine silver solder joint.
6 min	**End** 1 Recap over main points. Build up chalkboard from students answers. 2 Mention common errors (*a*) over heating (*b*) melting solder before job is warm enough. 3 Give notes from blackboard built up during the recapping stage. 4 State that the subject of silver soldering will be dealt with fully in the lecture room when joining of metals will be discussed. 　　Students to proceed to carry out the soldering exercise and submit it for inspection.

The demonstration is an essential feature in the teaching of cookery and catering subjects. It is important to order ingredients and prepare materials and equipment as well as to draw up a time schedule. The lesson plan which follows shows the detailed analysis required to ensure an accurate performance by the teacher and closely supervised student practice.

Subject: Rubbing-in method   *Class:* 147 City & Guilds   *Time:* 9.30 am–12 p

Background: Part-time   *No. of students:* 11

Lesson objectives

To teach:
1 The uses of scone and plain cake mixtures.
2 The rubbing in method using a small amount of fat.
3 The uses of raising agents of correct type and proportion.
4 The importance of consistency.
5 The importance of light handling.
6 The importance of baking.
7 Variations which can be applied to the Basic Method.

Stages and main points

Beginning

Introduction:

Characteristics of scone mixtures:

(1) small amount of fat, (2) lightness.

Teach by revision the types of raising agents and introduce the use of artificial raising agents for lesson by referring to visual aid.

Middle

Demonstration: scones, rock and raspberry buns	*Students' Practical*
1 Teach importance of correct oven temperature and preparation of baking sheets.	½ class – Cheese scones Rock buns
2 Teach sieving of flour incorporates air and makes for lightness.	½ class – Fruit Scones Raspberry Buns
3 Teach that artificial raising agents are used and refer to visual aid.	
4 Teach proportions of fat to flour.	*Points to Supervise*
5 Teach suitable fat to use.	Rubbing in of fat
6 Demonstrate "rubbing in" with finger tips.	Addition of liquid
7 Teach additions to basic mixture.	Rolling of dough
8 Demonstrate mixing lightly and quickly.	Cutting
9 Demonstrate rolling lightly to required thickness.	Baking
10 Teach to cut rounds close together to avoid waste.	Finish – Presentation Cleanliness – Tidiness
11 Demonstrate glazing with milk and refer to temperature and shelf of oven.	

Raspberry and Rock Buns

1 Teach that baking powder is used as raising agent.
2 Teach larger proportion fat to flour used than for scone mixture.
3 Revise basic rubbing-in method.
4 Add variations for flavouring.
5 Teach that egg is used as binder and gives extra food value.
6 Teach that consistency should be fairly stiff.

End

Summary: Use demonstration dishes and students' practical work as a basis for discussion and helpful criticism.

Refer to the "creaming" method for future lesson which can be used as the basis for biscuit making.

Time Plan

Introduction: 9.30 a.m.	Clearing up: 11.30 a.m.–11.50 a.m.
Demonstration: 9.33 a.m.–10.15. a.m.	Summary: 11.50 a.m.–12.00 p.m.
Students' Practical: 10.15 a.m.–11.30 a.m.	Questions, etc.

TEACHING A SKILL

Many skilled performances can be demonstrated. The manipulative aspects of a skilled performance can be observed by the student, but he needs to be given hints and cues at appropriate points in the performance. Hence the importance of verbal guidance and visual aids in enhancing the value of a demonstration. The amount of guidance given is important and *when* it is given. It is desirable to give guidance to the student as early as possible. The student's progress varies considerably with the type of skill being practised but with many skills the student will reach a stage at which little progress is made – the "plateau". He has not necessarily reached the peak of his performance but may progress subsequently to his "ceiling". The sequence of learning a skill is broadly indicated in the learning curve in Fig 9.1.

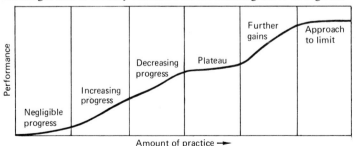

Fig 9.1 *General learning curve*

When a golfer sees his ball fall into the rough he is getting knowledge of results. Similarly when a student is told how well he is progressing in his practice he is receiving knowledge of results. Knowledge of results is important in promoting efficient learning and in maintaining high levels of performance. It can act as (*a*) a *reinforcer,* increasing the incidence or repetition of the correct performance and (*b*) an *incentive,* motivating effort through the promise of achievement and self-enhancement. Carefully spaced practice time is generally more beneficial than massed practice for the learning of a skilled performance.

ROLE-PLAY

This teaching method aims to give individual students insight into the ways in which organizations work and humans react. It has been app- lied mainly to management and supervisory training but may also be used to prepare students for a wide range of "situational" pressures. For example, a waitress in a busy restaurant is in a tense, highly- pressurized situation, at the focus of pressures from the head waiter, kitchen staff and barmen. Finally she is under pressure to attend to a constant flow of more customers, yet without neglecting those already eating. She can be taught a drill of priorities for dealing with new customers which enables her to control these pressures. But without it she breaks down in tears, and always at the busiest time. The training restaurant can place the student-waitress in a situation as realistic as possible and test her ability to apply knowledge she has gained in more formal teaching sessions.

   The differentiation of roles can be made acceptable to students of hotel and catering subjects by "working through" jobs in the bar, in the kitchen, and at the reception desk. People resist differentiation of roles; they fear that they will have some of their authority or their status filched from them. Role-play can illustrate how group pressure can make a person function well below his potential level. A high standard group can work the other way too, and bring a person up to a quite unexpected level. Role-play may be used to improve students' techniques of communication. A well-tried role- play exercise is the interview. If it is a selection interview, it could be aimed at improving the interviewer's reliability. Some guides are:

1 *Before* you start, decide just what you want to find out.
2 Don't try to get information from the interview that you can get by other means.
3 Start by having a definite pattern in the interview.
4 Watch for your own reactions to what the interviewer says.
5 Listen hard. *You* are assessing *him.* So make him talk, and then let him talk.

The playing-out of a situation is frequently linked with other informal teaching methods such as group discussion and case study.

GROUP DISCUSSION

The purposes of this teaching method are numerous:

1 To assist students in assimilating information received in more formal settings
2 To consider the solution of problems
3 To help students to recognize principles which may apply to many different situations.
4 To train students to organize their thoughts
5 To pool students' experiences

Secondary aims would be to develop students' ability to express an opinion in a reasonable tone of voice, and to listen to the views of others.

The optimum size for a group discussion appears to be between 8 and 15 students. This method offers plenty of scope for experiment with seating arrangements. Essentially the leader and each participant should be visible and audible to each other. The leader should be capable of preparing the topic for discussion, presenting it, ensuring that each member of the group takes part, and of summing up the main points raised. The methods of presentation are limited only by the ingenuity of the leader but usually he introduces the topic with a short talk, which can often make a greater impact if it is illustrated by some visual examples. On a course of teacher training a student-leader prepared the following notes and visuals to introduce a discussion of "Homework".

Discussion Topic

HOMEWORK

Aim
To discuss the place of Homework in the pattern of a modern education system with particular reference to Further Education in the 15–18 age groups.

HMI Inquiry
Subject of class teaching raises the problem of homework to which it is closely connected – 1937 Board of Education issued a pamphlet (No. 110) dealing with homework which was based on an inquiry carried out by HM Inspectorate.

It pointed out that homework had never been part of compulsory education but there had been an increasing tendency to set it – more in urban than rural areas – more in prosperous than distressed areas, but the most significant fact was that the demand for homework was almost always determined by reasons external to the school, i.e. an examination of some sort. Examples: 114, RSA, GCE, Entry to the Service Schools, etc.

Reasons

Most grammar schools have regular homework demands to cope with exams.

Modern and selective schools set homework because they believe the practice will raise their status nearer to that of the grammar.

As to its advisability, there seems to be a conflict of views among educationalists.

Some say that examination requirements make homework essentially desirable while some say that it is not – others claim that it is good training for students to acquire experience of working on their own initiative and not under the eye of teachers.

Outside Pressure

Parents often demand homework and consider the school slack if none is demanded – they want their children to be kept up to scratch and even driven in order to obtain exam results, others complain their offspring are overworked and write indignant letters to the press, again others leave things to the school.

Further education

Even in the old days almost every secondary day school contained a proportion of pupils who did homework under appalling handicaps, but the proportion of students between 15 to 18 attending further education courses who suffer such handicaps must be greatly increased. Even so, homework marks are part of most course results.

Drops 1 and 2

Is it reasonable to expect youngsters to work adequately at home when there is no place where they can be quiet, where there are several younger children, where the business of the family is going on around, where there is no cultural background, no books, no understanding of, or sympathy with the students' needs?

Dangers of homework

One of the main dangers in an organized homework system is that it may interfere with due leisure, recreation and opportunities for exercise in the open air. It may thus involve pressures on an adolescent at a time when such pressures are most to be deprecated.

The dangers involved in homework are most pronounced where the whole of the curriculum is influenced by the ultimate reward of passing an examination.

Drop 3

Fig 9.2 *Drop 1*

Fig 9.3 *Drop 2*

REWARD

CERTIFICATE OF SEC. EDUCATION

GCE

CITY & GUILDS CERTIFICATES

NATIONAL CERTIFICATES

DIPLOMAS

Fig 9.4 *Drop 3*

CASE-STUDY

The teaching of supervisory and management subjects has been closely associated with the case-study. A problem is presented, the teacher provides all the necessary information and leaves the group of students to discuss solutions to the problem. For example, a problem in personal relationships could arise from the case of the young worker whose first days at work are bedevilled by an unsympathetic journeyman and an incompetent chargehand.

A little forethought can provide useful case-studies for teachers of a far wider range of subjects. A group of occupational therapists could be given a referal form on a particular patient with a certain disease and its accompanying disabilities. Their assignment would be to study the case and plan a course of treatment with the ultimate aim of allowing or assisting this patient to return to his own home to live as independent a life as possible. The students would bear in mind the patient's occupation and ways in which sources of assistance might be tapped. The tutor would present supplementary information to fill out the students' knowledge and point out any snags which might not have occurred to the students. The aim of the case study would be to prepare students for clinical work, to explore every possible channel of assistance for patients, and to teach the students to respond to the patient's needs.

The case-study should provoke clear thinking about the set of facts presented either in a written case or in dramatized form (role-play or on film), so that students work out the underlying principles involved in the case, casting out irrelevant detail and testing and questioning each step.

TUTORIALS

The White Paper *Better Opportunities in Technical Education 1961* expressed concern about the large number of students who did not complete courses or failed to pass the examinations at the end of them. It suggested that improvements could be brought about by more individual attention to students. Greater efforts have since been made to foster informal relations between staff and students, to supplement and sometimes replace more formal lessons with the tutorial. The tutor meets students either individually, or in pairs or in larger groups. Only in the more advanced classes will the classical type of tutorial be practised — that is the duologue method which proceeds by cross-examination and pertinent rather than random interrogation. More often the tutor meets a group of students to:

1 Discuss an exercise or an essay.
2 Obtain feedback about the course.

3 Allow the students to do "homework".
4 Give the students an opportunity for private study.
5 Have students deliver prepared talks.
6 Provide for remedial teaching where necessary.

Too frequently tutorials degenerate into unstructured and purposeless periods. The teacher's difficulties relate to his lack of definite objectives or failure to occupy his students.

In a tutorial with students of catering the tutor may discuss the weekly exercise in menu compilation. He may broaden the practical work by developing from ideas of basic sauces to elaborate sauces, from simple ice-creams to parfaits and bombes. He may make references to modern kitchen accommodation and equipment and direct the students to appropriate magazines.

Moreover, the tutorial may be used to give individual attention to the student who has fallen behind in his studies because of illness, or to the student whose work has deteriorated because of some distraction, or to the student who needs constant encouragement and stimulation.

LIBRARY TUTORIAL WORK

The tutor-librarian is a post created at most colleges of further education. The appointee's main effort is given to the organization and day-to-day conduct of the business of the library. His remaining duties usually include the teaching of general studies and the introduction of a wide range of classes to the resources of the library. Only to a limited degree is he able to offer a systematic course in the use of the library to the majority of students. Norman Burgess of Bolton Technical College is the original *library-tutor,* whose duties are divorced from the responsibilities of running the college library but are concerned entirely with providing short tutorial courses to a variety of classes within the college. Burgess gives his aims as follows:

1 To demonstrate the importance of adequate recording of information and its subsequent communication.
2 To familiarize students with the use of books, periodicals and libraries.
3 To develop library tutorials as a teaching method.
4 To provide an opportunity for students to undertake individual work.

His methods will vary, naturally, according to the standard of the students and to the time available. There is a common core of information that should be given to all students:

1 The importance of information and its communication. The nature and size of the problem.
2 The records of information. Books, pamphlets, periodicals, film, tape, etc. Their sources.
3 The critical use of printed material. Judgement of the value of different sources of information.
4 The library.
5 Arrangement of material within a library. Classification. The catalogue.
6 The Librarians' tools. Bibliographies, Indexes, Abstracts.
7 Sources outside a particular library. Interloan services.

   Practical work can be designed to suit different student levels and may take one of three alternative forms:

1 A number of individual bibliographical assignments. Short tasks such as compiling book lists, assessing the merits and scope of a number of publications. Description of a publication — its scope and purpose. Tracing information on a certain subject. Finding the source of a statement.
2 Actual use of books and bibliographies likely to be met with in the subsequent careers of the students. Question set by tutor to be answered by use of specific reference books. Students may set their own questions to be answered by other members of the class.
3 A library project. A piece of written work for which the student prepares a reading list. He reads and selects material, prepares notes and composes an "integrated" essay or minor thesis. This may have a target of 5,000 words.

Within a group of eighteen engineering students a reasonably complete picture can be built of the history, pioneers and growth of the industry. The worker, trade unions, health and welfare services, government regulation of industry form another group of topics. A third group covers housing, town and country planning, the mass media and the use of leisure.

PROJECTS

A project should set the student the task of doing or making something; it should be distinguished from the extended essay or the study in depth. It may take various forms:

1 The investigation of a problem necessitating experiment, e.g. the design of experimental apparatus in an engineering subject or the design and administration of a questionnaire or survey with a social science class.

2 The construction of a piece of equipment or machinery.
3 The planning and layout of a process or product.

In an examination course the project should require the reading of background and associated literature, the planning of a course of action, a trial run and eventually the preparation of a report. In a non-vocational class in gardening one group could be given the project of reorganizing a potting shed, another group the construction of a rustic arch. The choice of design for the rustic arch could be made after each group member had submitted a scheme. The construction work could be broken down into units and assigned to individual students. They would work under supervision. The final erection would be a joint effort. To complete the project the group would discuss the problems of construction and erection of the arch, before presenting a report in their folios. The heads of assessment for the project would be:

1 Folio presentation.
2 Application (practical work).
3 Use of tools.

The problems of projects stem from (*a*) the amount of supervision required, (*b*) the availability of facilities and background literature, (*c*) marking the "results" of the work, whatever form they may take, (*d*) the assessment of the students' initiative and application. At best the group project can produce a spirit of co-operation beyond the scope of any other teaching method.

The project is often used as a "flux" to bring together the various components of a course. In an engineering course, it is sensible to get the student to employ what he has learned both in industry and in the course. By doing so he brings his skill and his experience to the service of the group, and teamwork is created. Tasks should be allocated to students who have the appropriate industrial training and experience. A project might require from a few weeks to some months, and could well involve preparatory drawing and design. The object should be to develop the ability to work together in a group, to plan, and to carry through the project to completion by proper use of time and facilities.

There are strategic points in most study programmes where the advantages to be gained from introducing project work are considerably enhanced. One example suitable for a small group (of, say, four students) on a joint project would be the reconditioning of a small machine. Such a project can involve the student emotionally and retain his interest.

VISITS

Ideally an educational visit should be organized to enlarge and illustrate a syllabus topic more tellingly than any other method available to the teacher. It should be timed to precede or follow the class coverage of the topic as closely as possible. A visit to a steel foundry would be a suitable follow-up to lessons on the casting of steel, foundry process and the use of castings. Background reading could cover the mining of ore, transportation to various foundries, as well as the stages in the treatment of the ore.

A visit should aim to foster and direct the student's curiosity and awaken his powers of observation. To derive maximum benefit a questionnaire or list of points for particular consideration should be drawn up. For a visit to a restaurant the check-list might take the following form:

INDUSTRIAL VISIT: RESTAURANT

1 *Pattern of Business:*

Daily-breakfast, luncheon, dinner/supper
Weekly
Annual
Functions

2 *Accommodation:*

Table content
Seating capacity

3 *Ownership:*

Public or private company, brewery, hotel group?

4 *Details of staff employed:*

	Males	Females
Full-time		
Part-time		
Totals		

5 *Kitchen:*

Number and grades of personnel
Equipment
Layout
Methods of service

6 *Supplies:*

Method of ordering and person responsible
Perishables
Groceries
Frozen, canned
Daily supplies to kitchen
Meat

7 *Deliveries:*

System of check on receipt

8 *Menus:*

Who plans them?
How is cost control executed?

9 *Business promotion:*

How is goodwill maintained?
How is business promoted?

INFORMAL METHODS

The methods described in this chapter are all departures from "two by four" teaching (two covers of a textbook; four walls of a classroom). They are generally linked to student activity and discussion. A further development is that of team teaching. There are various patterns of team teaching but one illustration would be:

1 100 students of business studies meet as a group; lecture from one teacher for 35 minutes.
2 Break into discussion groups, each with own tutor, discussion and amplification of content of lecture.
3 Work assignments on topic of lecture.

Advantages claimed for team teaching are that all students benefit from the best teacher on each topic of the syllabus. Face-to-face tutorials and discussion periods, directed study and practical periods are all organized to make best use of a group of teachers. Some teachers will be correcting students' work during large-group instruction and will be able to reduce the time-lag between submission and return of assignments.

FURTHER READING

Norman Burgess, "The Library and Liberal Studies", *Liberal Education* No. 4, July 1963

Jack Mansell, "Team Teaching: an analysis of students' views", *The Technical Journal* February 1970

Better Opportunities in Technical Education, 1961, Cmnd 1254 HMSO.

10
Teaching Aids

Visual and auditory illustrations have become an almost universal means of teaching. The use of carefully prepared and relevant aids can improve student achievement, but these aids need to be chosen in relation to (1) the students, (2) the subject matter and (3) the ways in which the subject matter is organized.

PERCEPTION

The five senses — sight, hearing, touch, smell and taste — are the student's points of contact with the outside world. They are his channels of communication to the brain. He learns by experience — through the senses. The senses may be said to include the "muscular" or "kinaesthetic" sense, which is concerned with the sensations of movement in the muscles, joints and tendons. The efficiency of these sensory channels varies with each student and is affected both by fatigue and by learning habits. Older students experience a slowing of their reaction time, that is the time that elapses between becoming aware of a situation, summing it up and making a decision. Students strive to impose a pattern or a structure or attach a meaning to any new experience or teaching material presented to them, whether it is a diagram, a theory or a sample of workmanship. Moreover, students do not always notice those items which appear to *us* to be important. Often they notice relatively unimportant details.

APPEAL TO THE SENSES

To accommodate students' individual differences in their use and preference of auditory and visual channels; the teacher should:

1 Make a balanced appeal to the senses by employing visual, oral, verbal and practical methods.
2 Change his tactics when students become tired — "tired of looking, start listening".
3 Explain what is happening; get students to talk about it until they show they grasp the significant features (in either moving or static illustrations)
4 Choose the category of media most appropriate to the content of the lesson.

TEACHING MEDIA
There are three main categories of audio-visual aids and media:

Teaching aids used by the teacher — chalkboard, filmstrips, slides, charts, diagrams, flannel board, magnetic board, plastigraph, models and samples.
Learning media used by the student — programmed books, teaching machines, film loops, self-instructional kits.
Mass communication media which originate outside the teaching establishment — sound broadcasts, educational television.

CHALKBOARD
The most usual and most versatile of visual aids is the chalkboard. Only one of the many functions of the overhead projector is as a substitute for the chalkboard. The chalkboard should be in occasional, if not in constant, use during an oral lesson. If the lesson is one of continuous exposition, each major point should be written down as it is established: so that at the end of the lesson the teacher would have before the class a brief but comprehensive summary of his major points. The lesson in the essential features of its anatomy will be before the student's eyes: and if the students make notes of the lesson obviously such a summary will be of the greatest assistance to them. The best way of constructing this chalkboard summary is to write during the lesson the points 1, 2, 3, 4, as these "points" emerge. Sometimes it is convenient to write up a summary before the lesson begins so that the class is informed beforehand of the aim of the lesson. Students often listen more intelligently if they know in outline what they are going to hear. At other times the chalkboard summary may be constructed during the vital process of recapitulation. If recapitulation takes the form of questioning, the chalkboard summary that is before the eyes of the students forms its most convenient basis.

In many lessons, however, particularly in those where the class, possibly after some preliminary explanation, is working individually from books, the chalkboard is best used incidentally to explain some process, some general error, which requires explanation to the class as a whole. Similarly, whenever terms have to be explained or unusual words come into use, they should be written down so that the visual memory of the students may be exercised.

There are certain elementary matters to consider in the use of the chalkboard:

1 Handwriting should be legible. Some advice on lettering is given in Fig 10.1.

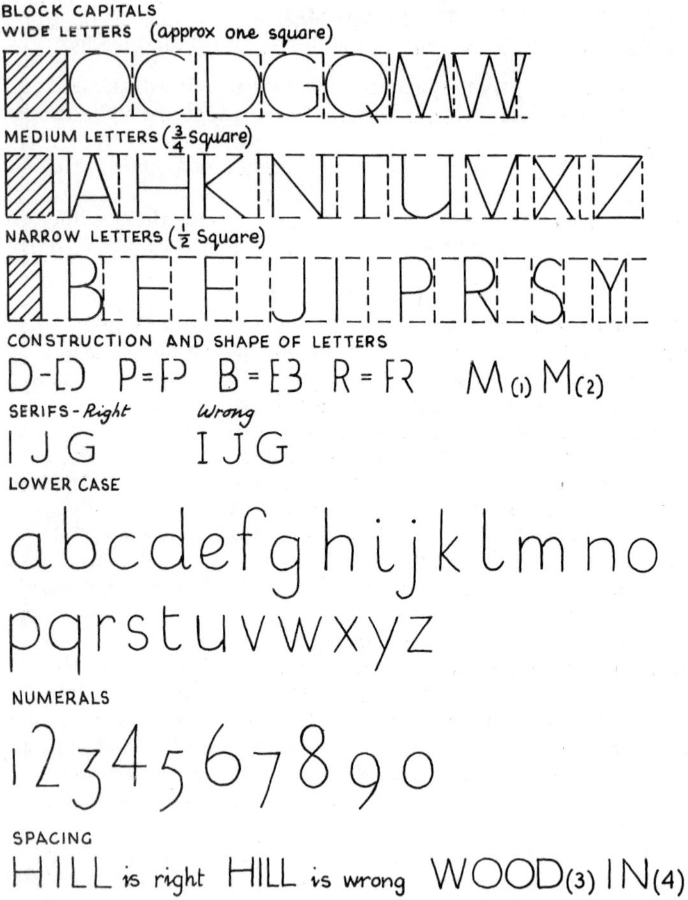

BLOCK CAPITALS
WIDE LETTERS (approx one square)

MEDIUM LETTERS ($\frac{3}{4}$ Square)

NARROW LETTERS ($\frac{1}{2}$ Square)

CONSTRUCTION AND SHAPE OF LETTERS

D-D P=P B=B R=R M(1) M(2)

SERIFS - *Right* *Wrong*

I J G I J G

LOWER CASE

abcdefghijklmno
pqrstuvwxyz

NUMERALS

1234567890

SPACING

HILL is right HILL is wrong WOOD(3) IN(4)

Fig 10.1 *Lettering*

2 If the chalkboard is a movable one it should be placed so as to be visible by *all* the students.

3 The matter written on the chalkboard should be orderly and tidy: It should be restricted to about 6 lines in any one unit.

4 What is written on it should be large enough to be seen by *all* students without strain. In the normal size of room the student may be 10 m from the board. Lettering should have a minimum capital letter height of 2 cm.

5 Colour should be used to emphasize important points. The aggressive colours, yellow and orange are best; the more restful blues, greens, browns and purples, do not "carry" so well.

Construction and Shape of Capitals. Notice construction of D, P, B, R, letters which are built up from semicircles.

The outside strokes of M(1) are not far from the vertical position. The inside strokes are more sloping. M(2) shows an alternative form.

Positions of Crossbars and Junctions. In H, K, X, B, E, F, Y, the position of crossbar or junction is just above the centre. In A, P, R, it is below the centre.

Serifs. Block lettering has NO SERIFS. Note especially I, J and G.

Relation of Capitals, Lower Case and Numerals. The first three lines of capitals, the lower case and the numerals on the sheet are drawn to the Same Scale. It will be seen that the body size of the lower-case letters and of the numerals is half the height of the capitals; that the lower-case letters and numerals with ascenders (e.g. b,2) are the same height as the capitals; that the descenders on lower-case letters are not quite as long as the ascenders (e.g. p, q, y); that the descenders on numerals are the same size as the ascenders (e.g. 4, 5). Note that "0" and "1" are the same height as lower-case "o", and that of the other figures the evens go above the line and the odds below.

Spacing: Of letters in a Word. The spacing of letters must be done by the judgement of the eye, *not* by measurement. In a well spaced word the *area* of space between letters is roughly equal, *not* the *distance* (see the word "HILL" in Fig 10.1). Useful rule: round letters should be close together (3), straight letters should be far apart (4).

Of words in a line. There should normally be the width of an "o" between words.

Of lines on a Panel. (*a*) Space between lines: for capitals this should be at least half the height of the letters; for lower-case letters, it is commonly twice the size of "o", though it can be less. (*b*) Margins: lettering and diagrams should have adequate margins all round. The tail margin is usually wider than the head and side margins.

SOME GENERAL PRINCIPLES

There is a wide range of mechanical and electronic teaching aids in use today in Further Education. The idea has gradually taken root that students themselves might make use of such equipment — film-strip and slide projector, cine film, radio and television, record-player, tape-recorder, language laboratory, programmed learning and teaching machine, and closed circuit television. For teachers who

seek guidance about the role of equipment and the systematic use of
techniques and aids, R T B Lamb's book, *Aids to Modern Teaching,*
is informative. There is no conclusive evidence that any one form of
visual aid is more effective than another. Each medium has unique
characteristics. Films may be used when motion and magnification
is required to convey manipulative tasks or processes. Still pictures
may be effective in place of films, when the teacher needs to stress
important points. Slides and filmstrip enable the teacher to increase
the time students may view illustrations, to answer their questions
and to make comments.

There is some general advice which can be advanced for using
visual illustrations effectively in conjunction with oral instruction. To
present students with the "real thing" — the process component, the
instrument or the apparatus — is not necessarily the best way of
transmitting information to students or of facilitating their learning.

It would appear that visuals closely representing line drawings and
containing the essence of the information to be transmitted would be
more effective and more efficient in facilitating learning than would
more detailed illustrations. Fig.10.2 shows in simplified form how
alternating current carries information from the studio through the
transmission system, over the air to the radio set, and then through
the set to the loudspeaker and finally from the loudspeaker to our
ears.

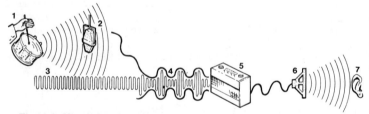

Fig 10.2 *Visual showing course of information from the studio to the ear*
1, drum; 2, microphone; 3, radio transmitter; 4, modulated wave;
5, radio set; 6, loudspeaker; 7, ear

EDUCATIONAL TECHNOLOGY

Technology may be described as the science of the application of
knowledge to practical purposes, so educational technology is a way
of applying available knowledge of equipment and materials (resource
media) and teachers and supporting technicians, in a systematic

manner to problems of education and training. Efficiency and cost-effectiveness are currently pursued by the administrators of further education. These two objectives may ultimately be achieved by introducing teachers to (i) the range of resources offered by educational technology and (ii) the idea of planning educational systems to make effective use of manpower, materials and money in education.

FURTHER READING

Learning and Teaching Tomorrow Occasional Paper No 2 (16 pages), from National Council for Educational Technology, 160 Great Portland Street, London W 1

D H Holding *Principles of Training,* 1965, Chapter 4 "Visual Methods" pages 54−67

11

Breadth in Teaching

The Government White Paper *Technical Education* (1956) gave impetus to the broadening of the teaching of subjects in further education in these words:

". . . and more attention will have to be given to the teaching of good plain English, the use of which saves time and money and avoids trouble. . . . Moreover a place must always be found in technical studies for liberal education . . . a wide treatment of scientific and technical subjects is essential if students who are to occupy responsible positions in industry are to emerge from their education with a broad outlook. We cannot afford either to fall behind in technical accomplishments or to neglect spiritual and human values".

In the last ten years we have gone a long way in the introduction of liberal elements into further education and in employing a variety of methods of broadening teaching objectives. Considerable success has attended experiments such as short residential courses, arts societies, informal discussions and film studies in giving liberal studies a relevance to modern living.

EXTENDING THE SUBJECT

So far we have been concerned with the principle of limiting the teaching objective at each precise stage of the lesson or the teaching programme, and with the conveying of information, basic skills, techniques and methods. There is also the complementary principle of extending the basic techniques of a craft or technology into aesthetics, design and social values. The teacher of medical laboratory science can extend his treatment of such topics as genetic code, cell replication and reproduction to the power of science and technology to change the quality of life – for good or evil. In the hairdressing class the teacher can move from the cutting, thinning and shaping of hair to a discussion of hair styles for different occasions in different environments, to the sociological aspects of uni-sex styles, to the selection of colours and the harmonizing and contrasting of shades. In non-vocational classes a subject such as dressmaking could be taken beyond the teaching of the techniques of button-holing, drafting and stitching to the effectiveness of the finished garment, to the amount of creativity put into it, to questions of taste and judgement.

The publication in 1957 of Circular 323 by the Ministry of Education marked the official declaration that liberal teaching should be practised in further education; in the first instance by changing the organization of technical studies and adopting new methods of treatment of those studies. Such changes have been made in many syllabuses and teaching schemes. To take one example, in a course for craft students in the printing industry, the syllabus for printing techniques and materials contains a section on "A Survey of the Printing Industry":

Location and size.
Brief historical development.
Modern trends.
Apprentices — selection — relation with journeymen — trade unions.
Autonomy and demarcation.

The teaching method comprises exposition by the teacher, visits to local printing establishments and students, directed reading. A questionnaire is given to each student which provides a basis for individual work; the following provide examples of the questions:

1 Produce two comparable bar charts showing the sizes of printing companies in terms of employment and the number of establishments in each category.
2 Why does the small firm need to specialize and what does this involve?
3 What are the responsibilities of the employer towards the apprentice?
4 Give the aims of the Industrial Training Board and those of Further Education.
5 What are the reasons for scientific research in the printing industry?

LIBERAL OR GENERAL STUDIES

Circular 323 also suggested the addition of other subjects to those of vocational interest. The intention was that these additional subjects should "act and interact with the technical studies to produce a well-informed, discriminating and tolerant person". Liberal studies have become not so much a subject or an injection of culture to cure people of technical fever: they are more an attitude and an approach. There are no liberal studies as such, only liberal teaching. Every subject, whether it is drawing, mathematics or moulding, should be taught liberally to help students:

1 To see links with wider things.
2 To know not just how something works but why.
3 To raise questions of value as well as to describe.
4 To make excursions from their immediate working environment.
5 To see what goes on outside their place of employment and what
   spare-time activities they can take part in.

One well-tried method of teaching "liberal studies" is to start with
the student's job and to broaden his knowledge of developments in
his industry. A topic of immediate concern is metrication. The lesson
plan given below provides time for informal discussion and visual
illustration in the form of a film that gives heightened interest because
it features a local factory and its scheme for tackling metrication.

Subject and level: Liberal Studies (3rd Year)   *Class:* CGLI Sheet Metalwork
                                                          (3rd Year)
Textbooks: British Standards Pamphlet   *Background:* Two-Year Craft

No. of students: 17   *Time:* 11.00 am–12.00 pm

LESSON OBJECTIVES

1 To introduce changeover from existing "imperial" system of measurement,
   to the new SI unit system.
2 To examine, briefly, the advantages and problems of the changeover.

LESSON PLAN

Time	Stages and Main Points	Aids
	Beginning	
11.03	1 A time of changing traditions, customs and systems. 2 The need for change in international trading. Changing markets. 3 Involvement of industry and worker.	Chalkboard
	Middle	
11.10	1 Define the new SI system. 2 Changeover expected by 1975. 3 Main advantage of new system in work and production. 4 Illustrate the six basic units of measurement in SI system. 5 Outline of problems facing industry. 6 Examples of (5) to be illustrated by visual aid.* 7 Question arising from film. * Class will transfer to Projection Room, for film.	Film: "Going Metric" produced by BBC

End
1 Confederation of British Industry (CBI) campaign.
2 Future possibilities for trade as members of European Economic Community.
3 Changing syllabuses in schools and colleges.

The subject matter for liberal studies might be evolved from such subjects as the responsibilities of the new wage-earner, and the cost of setting up a home. A number of agencies such as National Savings Committee provide suggestions for syllabus expansion. The following area of knowledge is offered as an example of how a unit might be organized.

Budgeting

1 *National Budget* – Revenue and expenditure – Social Services.
2 *Local Authority Budget.*
Class Project: Students to examine the local rate demand note and discuss items of expenditure.
Suggested Outside speaker: Treasurer of Local Authority.

3 *Personal Budget*
  (i) Pocket Money – compared to wages.
 (ii) Personal Budget – necessary to control expenditure and ensure money available for essentials.
(iii) Difference between essentials and near-essentials – non-essentials and luxuries. Need to maintain a wise balance between those items.
(iv) Preparing a personal Budget – for dividing up the money, e.g. board and lodging, fares, clothes, holidays, weekly expenses and entertainment, saving for emergencies, presents, etc.
 (v) Living at home – making a fair contribution; learning about the family budget, doing the shopping.
(vi) Boy meets Girl – sharing the cost of outings; "going steady"; planning ahead,
(vii) The family budget; housekeeping and home expenditure.

Class Projects: Student to prepare:
A list of all items on which they now spend money.
A list of the extra items on which they will have to spend money when they start their own home.
A personal budget based on a wage of £12 per week for a young person living at home, working locally with mid-day meal at a canteen.
A family budget for a family of four, income £25.

PROBLEMS OF BROADENING

The liberalizing movement has produced an impressive array of subjects, projects and activities, often in spite of (1) the students' weak motivation in these subjects, (2) lack of co-operation from many teachers who are doubtful of their value and (3) the indifference of employers. Liberal Studies teachers have been "conned" by the name game and have created their own problems in producing such terms as "complementary", "contrasting", "humanistic" and "personal" studies. They are a far cry from the class of thirty tough Motor Vehicle chaps who have to be kept interested late every Friday afternoon. A T G Edwards, a pioneer of "Breadth in the Technical College", offers a balanced point of view in his valedictory:

"Although the anonymous author of the recent *Guardian* onslaught, 'Liberal Studies, Liberal Humbug', was as guilty as those he attacked of dwelling on *what* to the exclusion of *how* and *why,* there was one point where he touched on the heart of the matter. 'How many teachers themselves', he asked, 'are walking examples of what they expect their students to become?' That surely is the crux: there are no liberal studies (i.e. liberalizing subjects) as such; only liberal (i.e. liberating) teaching. Once this is admitted, a liberal education can be correctly seen not as a number of 'cultural disciplines' but as an attitude — an attitude that has something to do with raising blinds and opening windows, and with the free play of mind, and with pursuing the ramifications of *any* subject in ever-widening contexts of experience."

FURTHER READING

Beryl Harding *Ten Years of General Studies,* 1969 (85 pages), Association for Liberal Education
General Studies, 1970 (34 pages), City and Guilds of London Institute

REFERENCE

A T G Edwards *Memoirs from Beyond the Tomb,* valedictory piece, Coventry Technical College, July 1969, unpublished

12

Class Management

"There are two ways of reaching stability: by making rules initially and modifying them later or by having few rules and making more if they prove necessary." (Lord James of Rusholme.)

The whole art of teaching consists in helping students to learn in the way that is most economical of time and effort. Most students in further education desire to learn. The teacher should do all he can to support and reinforce that desire. The creation and maintenance of interest is the central task of the teacher. He should go about his work in a serious, businesslike, purposeful way and he will have little trouble with class management. Students will frequently respect a teacher's knowledge and sincerity even if he lacks presence and personality. However, an increasingly large number of students are exposed to further education through no wish of their own. Programmes of initial training promoted by the Industrial Training Boards, as well as courses of retraining made necessary by technological change and the de-skilling of crafts, create a crop of unwilling students, attending courses of further education only because it is a condition of employment.

It would be unjust to exaggerate the difficulties of managing classes in further education as it would be to ignore the poor standards of conduct and work of a minority which can develop a situation militating against good teaching. This can take the form of classroom misbehaviour, challenge to the teacher's authority, litter, careless work, failure to complete work set or damage to equipment. In a society that is increasingly permissive, youth tends to be less tolerant of authority than previous generations. Further education has its share of students who have a permanent "chip on the shoulder" and have acquired a resentment against all forms of authority.

MOTIVATIONS

Motivations – the driving forces of students – are much more complex than simple needs for food, shelter and sleep. Needs beyond these purely physiological ones are *learned*. They are learned from the cultural background via parents, friends and teachers. The basic need is security. Security is based on people. We know some of the effects on a child of breakdown in relationships in a family — of failure of that basic security. Social significance, feeling of belonging, is as important in further education as in employment and the home. Other needs, all linked with security, are for prestige in the eyes of those with whom one is emotionally identified; approval by those one wants to be approved by; praise for past efforts is more effective than any kind of correction. Another need is for some "control", e.g. going one's own pace, choosing the method of work. We tend to take this away from students. To "lose face" is unpleasant. Yet it seems childish to resent it. So students bottle up resentment. If they do, it breaks out in some other form. Reaction to frustration is not always direct. Aggression is the commonest reaction; but it can take the form of being rough with tools, botching work, criticizing the teacher behind his back. Another reaction is to revert to "childish" or illogical or unreasonable behaviour. The final stage is general apathy. The teacher's basic managerial skill is to see through the "latent" content of the students' speech and behaviour. The teacher need not look for deeper meanings in everything but he would be a fool to imagine that deeper meanings do not exist. Until the teacher sees that the students' frustration exists he cannot attempt to "transfer" it.

STUDENTS IN GROUPS

The student's attitudes, needs, how he sees things, are structured by the fact of belonging to a certain group: or, of course, being rejected by the group. In teaching we deal with "persons-in-a-group". Being a member of a group, "belongingness", has many advantages. Students will sacrifice a lot in order to conform or to "belong". Belonging — having a known place in a functioning social group — is the basis of security, and of self-respect. The power of the group is enormous. Relatively little has been done to make the most of the tremendous potential that lies in group work. "Participation" experiments are the exception in most courses. Teachers should try to make more use of the team spirit they often talk about. The teacher should not be afraid of losing status by forgoing the lecture or lesson form and allowing students to exert their own controls, through group projects and investigations.

DISCIPLINE AND ORDER

Good discipline in the sense of securing the order that alone makes teaching possible is not merely an aid to teaching. It is the condition precedent. Without it there can be neither teaching nor learning. Good teaching and good discipline go together, and, in the sense that the second of these is the direct result of the first, good teaching is good discipline.

In an attempt to answer the question "What do we mean by discipline?" Michael Duane has pointed out that we refer to the discipline of

(*a*) A well-trained regiment.
(*b*) An Olympic swimming team.
(*c*) A monastic order.
(*d*) The London Symphony Orchestra.

In (*a*), (*b*), (*c*) and (*d*) we are speaking of adults conscious of certain purposes and accepting the rigours of appropriate training – they accept a common code. When we speak of discipline in further education, it is idle to assume that students find such a common code acceptable. Group and individual discipline exists when students recognize that rational and democratic ways are being used in working for commonly agreed purposes.

Some leading principles, however, are useful in dealing with classes. There are three factors involved in class management:

1 The organizational aspect (order).
2 The teaching aspect.
3 The personal aspect (discipline).

ORGANIZATION

The arrangement of desks in parallel has its advantages but reminds students too vividly of school attendance, and it is wise to create the impression of a class being composed of "students" and not of "pupils". Therefore, an "arc" arrangement might be tried: it subtly suggests a more intimate relationship between teacher and taught.

Lighting should be considered in the arrangements of desks and tables so that there is a minimum amount of shadow falling upon the notebooks, textbooks, or material in use. The ventilation of the room should also be considered in relation to the desk and bench arrangement. A clean chalkboard, without slime, that can be clearly seen by all students is the teacher's responsibility.

It is particularly important in the case of Mechanical Drawing, Art, Needlework, Cookery and Craft classes to tell students in advance of the clothing and equipment needed and to insist on all having it. In practical classes the teacher should develop a routine for the sharing of duties in the distribution and collection of equipment and materials, so as to avoid the disorder which can result from an "every man-for-himself" attitude. If students are in difficulties it is better for the teacher to go to them. The class coming out to the teacher can create chaos. A climate helpful to purposeful learning can be engendered by ensuring that students enter and leave a room in orderly fashion.

TEACHING ASPECTS

Most students respond to praise and encouragement. The teacher should not be too sparing of these, for they produce a better atmosphere, even if they are not fully deserved. To create and maintain interest does not necessarily mean to be lively, or to attempt to be witty or dramatic for the purpose of temporarily arresting attention. To arouse and maintain interest the *oral* lesson must be clear. This means that teachers should have thought out how they are going to put their points. They must be sufficiently simple to be intelligible. Above all they must make even their oral lessons as co-operative as they can, carrying the classes with them, and enlisting their active participation at every opportunity.

Wherever it is possible, they must reduce class teaching to a reasonable limit, for every class will be heterogeneous in its composition. The rate of progress possible to its individual members will vary very much. It is vital that the able shall be allowed to go their pace and equally important that the less able shall be allowed to go more slowly. Wherever, therefore, individual methods can be followed, they should be followed, though the collective treatment of some points is bound to be necessary. Where, as sometimes will be the case, the subject must be taken forward lesson by lesson by the whole class, then the abler students must be encouraged to do more than the normal number of examples of more than ordinary difficulty. Whenever possible, too, it is advisable to divide a class into sections: but this is a matter of considerable difficulty to all except experienced teachers.

PERSONAL ASPECTS

Discipline cannot be imposed from without. Teachers have no sanctions, in the form of punishment, with which they can enfore their authority. They are thrown back upon their own personality and character. Many are reluctant to acknowledge that they have problems in managing classes since it appears to reflect on their professional ability.

It has been said that the teacher should possess the qualities of Jesus Christ, Socrates and Sir Laurence Olivier. He should be more than an actor, more approachable than a priest, and a humanitarian. Such high ideals cannot but lead the teacher to despair. However, he can temper his approach to classes in the knowledge that most students have a tendency to imitate and a wish to conform, which should assist him in the attitude he strikes to the class as a whole and in persuading individuals to identify themselves in the organization of class control. Students will learn unwittingly to take their cue from the teacher's personal example.

Above all the teacher should be consistent in his attitude to a class, sympathetic to students' problems — educational, occupational and personal. Some leading principles are:

1 Be friendly, good-humoured and easily approachable. Work out the most effective mode of addressing students.
2 Be firm and fair: let justice appear to be done with the support of the class.
3 Establish close contact with classes by questioning, and by looking them straight in the eye.
4 Have respect for students' opinions even if they are wrong. Never snub the honest asker or answerer of a question.
5 Always be well prepared, and, if possible, rehearsed. A teacher's love of and enthusiasm for his subject are contagious.
6 Adopt an air of not expecting trouble. Formulate few rules but let students know where they stand and what your "margin of toleration" is.
7 Spot potential trouble-makers. Deal with students individually, for instance, see awkward students privately to give them an opportunity to back down.

RECAPITULATION

Student behaviour is the outcome of the interaction of many factors. Some that are important to bear in mind are:

The cultural background of the society
The physical environment
Attitudes
Motivations
Physical and intellectual endowment
Situational pressures

Some of these are linked; some are different ways of saying the same thing. Often a class management problem involves all of them. The first step in tackling a "human relations" problem is to look at the situation as a whole, standing away from it as if one were a visitor from Mars.

Don't expect human behaviour to be rational or sensible. It is, of course; but it may be rational in terms of a different rationality from one's own. Don't expect to find a single panacea, any more than you would expect to find one "wonder-drug" to cure all diseases. It is not unimportant to have enough self-knowledge to know just how much you have yourself affected the classes you are managing.

FURTHER READING

Michael Argyle *The Psychology of Interpersonal Behaviour*, 1967, Chapter 9 (pages 150–80), Pelican Books

REFERENCE

Michael Duane "Parents and Discipline", *The Sunday Telegraph,* April 25, 1965

13

Testing and Assessing

TESTING AS A TEACHING INSTRUMENT

Testing is a teaching instrument when it tells the teacher what he is doing well and what he needs to do better; when it tells the student the result of his responses to the test. The setting of course work should aim to teach and to test students' application. The marking of course work requires that the teacher communicates the result in a way that the student appreciates — a numerical score or a lettered grade or a comment or extended criticism with or without an oral remark. A test — which should always relate to the object of the teaching — may be used at the end of each lesson, of each unit of work, and at the end of a term. It is unprofitable to submit students to lengthy written examinations until there is a range of information wide enough to convey to the students that their progress is worth the time given to testing it.

The students' results in examination tests may not give an efficient assessment of all sides of their work over a long period of time, maybe over the whole of the course. For this reason, many examinations are now being organized to require:

1 A record of course work — written work, practical tasks under-taken for study purposes — to be kept for each student.
2 A teacher's assessment based upon oral work in class, group activities or tutorials or discussions arranged during the course.

Teachers will be required increasingly to plan course assignments and tests, mark them and record the results.

ASSIGNMENTS AND HOMEWORK

It is impossible for a student to obtain any mastery of any subject without collateral study. With full-time classes a good deal of this can be done at the study centre or college. In part-time classes there is little time for individual study. Even in the conditions of a full-time course homework is usually justified, if only because it is profitable for the student to attempt some part of his work where help is not available. In part-time classes the setting of homework in reasonable quantity is an essential part of the teacher's art.

Two principal considerations are important. The homework should consist of the kind of work that can be done as well at home as in class — or even better; and it should never be excessive in quantity. Wherever the working of examples is desirable, or when practice is necessary, these examples, or exercises in the practice that gives facility, should be given as homework. In mathematics, for example, liberal use of examples or practice on given principles is most desirable. Homework when set should be marked, not always in great detail, but at least enough to prevent the perpetuation of major errors, and to satisfy the students that what they have done (or failed to do) has been noted by the teacher. The most profitable and beneficial type of homework is that which is concerned with what has been taught in the classroom, workshop or laboratory.

Homework need not always be written. Students should be encouraged to devote some of their spare moments to *thinking* out the answers to questions and problems which have arisen during the lessons. An oral rendering of these at subsequent meetings of the class can be a very valuable form of homework. A lesson may reasonably begin by the general oral examination of the preparation set.

ABILITIES TO BE TESTED

Broadly, course work assignments will test three abilities in the student

1 Remembering.
2 Understanding.
3 Thinking.

Above all the course work which the student submits should indicate the extent of his learning and his application. The teacher should be quite clear about the object of each item of course work, about the abilities and activities that are being called into play. B S Bloom in the *Taxonomy of Educational Objectives* has listed the following abilities that students might exhibit as a result of the learning process:

1 *Knowledge* — the ability to recall facts and practical techniques
2 *Comprehension* — the ability to translate data from one form to another (verbal into mathematical or graphical or vice versa); to interpret or deduce the significance of data; to solve problems in which the mode of solution should be familiar (to calculate)
3 *Application* — the ability to apply knowledge, experience and skill to new situations
4 *Analysis* — the ability to break down the elements of presented material, recognizing their relations and organization
5 *Synthesis* — the ability to put together elements and parts to form a whole

6 *Evaluation* — the ability to make a judgement as to the value of information in terms either of internal or of external criteria.

THE ESSAY FORM

The essay provides a good test of management whether it is set as an assignment or as a test. It tests the students' self-management, the organization of his time, ability to summarize material and the ability to present it economically and intelligently. It may also elicit originality and creativity. Too frequently — but often justly — the essay exercise has been accused of inviting the student to "marshalling ignorance" and "constructing vapidity". To test subject knowledge the essay must have a factual background. The following principles are devoted to these ends: to making the wording of questions less vague and the marking of the answers more analytic rather than impressionistic:

1 Define precisely the direction and scope of the answers desired — the worst offender among essay questions is the invitation to discuss something, e.g. "Discuss Local Authorities".

2 Provide a number of questions each of which demands a short answer, e.g.
   What is meant by a "Local Authority"?
   What is the largest type of Local Authority in terms of population?
   Which two factors influence the services a Local Authority provides?
   Why is local government likened to big business?
   Who operates the various services provided?
   In which authorities do you find (*a*) a Lord Mayor, (*b*) a Mayor, (*c*) a Chairman?
   What does a Chief Officer do?

3 Prepare a tentative scoring key, at the time of constructing the essay question, indicating the essential points in the answer, the number of marks to be awarded to each point, and the total to be awarded to the question.

EXAMPLE

Question: In not less than five hundred and fifty words consider the relative advantages and disadvantages of renting or buying a house. In addition, state what you understand to be the princiapl functions of a building society. How do present-day building societies differ in organization from the original societies?

Marking Scheme   *Total 20 marks*

A. Advantages and Disadvantages
1 *Renting a Property*
   (*a*) Lengthy wait for houses, especially in towns
     and cities.   ½
   (*b*) In privately rented accommodation, the risk
     of notice to quit.   ½
   (*c*) After years of paying rent, property is never
     one's own.   ½   2½
   (*d*) Choice of locality seldom possible.   ½
   (*e*) To pay rent and save is difficult.   ½

2 *Buying a Property*
   (*a*) Property eventually becomes free of debt.   ½
   (*b*) A permanent security unlikely to devalue.   ½
   (*c*) Locality restricted only by price range of
     property.   ½   2½
   (*d*) Freedom to sell and move.   ½
   (*e*) Income-tax relief allowed against mortgage
     interest repayments.   ½

B. Two-fold function of building societies:
   (*a*) To attract investment (saving) of capital by
     offering attractive rates of interest   3
   (*b*) To "re-direct" invested capital into loans
     (mortgages) for house purchase and earn interest
     for the invested capital   3

C. Building Societies
1 *Earliest Societies* were formed and operated to satisfy
small groups of prospective house-owners who "pooled"
their own savings in a group building scheme, allocating
each house by ballot or extra premium until all members
were housed.   1
2 *Today's building societies*
   (*a*) Not involved in process of building houses.   ½
   (*b*) Are legally constituted by Act of Parliament.   ½
   (*c*) Are "permanent" as distinct from "terminating"
     societies.   ½   2
   (*d*) Must make all accounts public under jurisdiction
     of the Registrar of Friendly Societies.   ½

D. General Layout — logical organization of material   3
E. Paragraphing   2
F. Punctuation and Spelling   1

                  Total 20

DIAGNOSTIC TESTING

It is a useful practice to encourage students to check their own work by means of a diagnostic test. An inspection of the student's answers shows (1) where the student does not yet know the right thing to do (2) the need for finding the cause of each error and (3) the need for remedial material.

After a lesson on the "Decimal Currency Shop", students were given a test presented so that they could check their answers by sliding a "mask" down the right-hand side of the test sheet, to reveal the answer to each test item.

EXAMPLE: Test: *Decimal Currency Shop* £ p

Goods offered at 7p. Customer has 5p and some £s.d.
Tenders 5p and 6d. What change is due to him?

Price of goods £3.59. Customer hands over £3.55 leaving 4p to find. Tenders 5p (1s) to receive?	½p
Price £3.03. Customer hands in £3, what sum in £sd must be tendered?	1p
What change will be received?	1s. (5p)
Articles 24p. Customer hands in 2 x 10p leaving 4p to find. He tenders 1s. and receives?	2p
Articles cost £1.39. Customer hands in 30s. What change does he receive?	1p
Goods cost 16p. Customer hands in 10p and 5p. No more new pence. What amount must he tender?	11p
What change is received?	6d (2½p)
Goods amount to 31p. Customer has 3 x 10p but but no more new pence. Offers 6d. What change due?	1½p
Articles cost £1.29½. Customer tenders £1, 2 x 10p and 5p leaving 4½p to find. Offers a sum of 1s and receives ___ p?	½p
Goods cost £4.73. Customer has £4, 1 x 50p, 1 x 10p and 1 x 5p. To find the 8p required what sum must be offered and what change is received?	2s. to receive 2p

OBJECTIVE TESTING

"An objective test may be defined as a series of items, each of which has a predetermined correct answer so that subjective judgement in the marking of each item is eliminated."

The objective-type test with its large numbers of short items makes for a more systematic coverage of the area of the syllabus to be examined than is possible with a briefly worded essay question. It avoids the drawbacks of illegible handwriting and can indicate the type or amount of lecture material successfully retained. It can test factual knowledge and the application of principles.

To compile an objective-type test the teacher must be able to define the aims of his teaching so that he can fit the test to the aims of the teaching. He should analyse in detail the subject matter the student should have been taught before compiling a large number of short items based on the topic analysis. To illustrate the procedure the following example gives (1) an extract from a syllabus derived from the regulations for the Electrical Equipment of Buildings, (2) an analysis of the topic, (3) an objective-style test on the theoretical knowledge of the topic. A practical test would, in addition, be required to test the ability to do the jobs specified.

SYLLABUS CONTENT DERIVED FROM THE ELECTRICAL EQUIPMENT OF BUILDINGS

Syllabus Content	Knowledge	Remembering	Application
Section A: Control distribution and excess current protection	1 Aware of cable size	Load it will carry	Correct type fuse
	2 Aware of reasons for fuse rating	Load circuit will carry	Correct type fuse
	3 Appropriate floor area	Not to exceed load	Complete installation
	4 Load of appliances	Fuse to accommodate load	Correct type fuse
	5 Limit of total load	Check load	Correct fuse and cable
	6 Load and performance of motor	Not to over-fuse	Check running and efficiency of motor
	7 Domestic types of load	Differences between industrial and domestic	Check load
	8 Of complete range	Types of voltage being worked on	Take precautions, aware of dangers, working conditions

Q1 Give the Electrical Board Authorities fuse cut-out size protecting the consumer's supply in domestic premises from the following:

(*a*) 30 Amp.
(*b*) 80 Amp.
(*c*) 60 Amp.
(*d*) 45 Amp.

Q2 From the list of alternatives below, give the fuse rating which protects a complete domestic ring main circuit:

(*a*) 10 Amp.
(*b*) 5 Amp.
(*c*) 15 Amp.
(*d*) 30 Amp.

Q3 In domestic premises an unlimited amount of socket outlets may be installed within a certain floor area, indicate which:

(*a*) 1,000 sq ft.
(*b*) 10,000 sq ft.
(*c*) 100 sq ft.
(*d*) 500 sq ft.

Q4 Fused plug tops are used in a ring main circuit. From the list below indicate the cartridge fuse range used for the connecting of various appliances:

(*a*) 5, 10, 15 Amp.
(*b*) 3, 7, 13 Amp.
(*c*) 2, 5, 10 Amp.
(*d*) 10, 13, 15 Amp.

Q5 From the list below give the amperage limit of total current demand on a fused spur as permitted on a ring main (cable size being same CSA as ring main installation):

(*a*) 5 Amp.
(*b*) 10 Amp.
(*c*) 20 Amp.
(*d*) 15 Amp.

Q6 Indicate size of conductor used in a domestic ring main installation from the following:

(*a*) 1·0 mm².
(*b*) 1·5 mm².
(*c*) 2·5 mm².
(*d*) 4·0 mm².

Q7 Give the maximum number of sockets allowed on a radial circuit installation other than domestic premises:

   (*a*) <u>6.</u>

   (*b*) 2.

   (*c*) unlimited.

   (*d*) 10.

Q8 From the various voltage ranges, indicate from the list given the medium voltage range:

   (*a*) Up to and including 50V.

   (*b*) Above 50V but not exceeding 250V.

   (*c*) <u>Above 250V but not exceeding 650V.</u>

   (*d*) Normally exceeding 650V.

Hostility to objective-type tests has arisen because most of the tests have tested the learning of snippets of information. However, test items can be devised to test understanding and organization of knowledge, of subject areas which do not permit of an absolutely right or wrong answer. The following extract illustrates how the true-false type item may be used in a subject where decisions or value-judgements have to be made in the light of reported evidence:

Topic: Perinatal Diseases

Instructions: Consider each of the following statements in relation to the history and then mark against each statement:

   T if the statement is more *true* than false

   F if the statement is more *false* than true

Please leave blank rather than guess the answer.

                                        T or F

Question 1 — A sheep farmer requests advice following six ewes aborting during the past week.

1 Assume the cause is infectious until proved otherwise.

2 The most likely infections are salmonella, vibrio, enzootic abortion virus, bisterella.

3 The aborting ewes should be isolated.

4 The laboratory needs foetuses, membranes and bloods from the six aborted ewes.

5 If none of the six ewes is ill, infectious abortions are less likely.

TESTING PRACTICAL ABILITY

The written test of the essay-type or the objective-type is not suitable for all purposes. There is a wide range of educational objectives — performing a skill, speaking a foreign language, working with materials and tools — which cannot be assessed directly by a written test.

The first step in constructing a test of practical ability is to define the activities or abilities to be tested. In a course of nurse-training an exercise might be arranged to test these activities: setting of medicine trolley and dismantling the trolley, administering of medicines orally, storing medicines with particular reference to replacement of keys.

The second step is to break down the task or exercise into elements so that each element may be scored separately to provide a mark scheme. One element could be, in this instance, the requirements for the trolley-tray:

		Mark
1	Tray.	1
2	Medicine glasses, oil cup, glass rods.	3
3	Jug of water.	1
4	Receivers for clean and used spoons and rods.	1
5	Bowl of hot water.	1
6	Medicine cloth.	1
7	Medicines.	1
8	Medicine list/chart.	1
	Total	10

For some exercises it is possible to make the test objective by providing a structured mark scheme for the product of the student's activities. For example in bread-making the loaf produced by each student could be assessed under the following heads:

General appearance:
   Crust Break
   Comb Definition

Symmetry

Volume

Crust:
   Bloom
   Colour

Crumb:
   Colour
   Texture
   Grain
   Pile
   Moistness
   Aroma
   Flavour

Weight

CONTINUOUS ASSESSMENT

Teachers act as assessors as part of their normal work. If a teacher
has decided that student X has made a better set of dentures than
student Y, he must have made a comparative assessment, based upon
evidence. This evidence becomes available as the teacher observes his
students in learning situations — remembering facts or applying
principles or performing skills. The judgement made by the teacher
may determine the amount of help and the kind of help to be given
to student Y. The recording of assessments of students' attainment
over the duration of a course is becoming one of the many tasks
which the teacher is obliged to undertake. Continuous or progressive
assessment measures changes in the students' performance. It is possible for the teacher to note improvement or deterioration in
performance; to use the evidence diagnostically, and as a result appropriate treatment may be applied.

Course work may take the form of exercises completed during
class time or as homework; it may be a project, or a personal study,
or an operational skill. Continuous assessment may take into account
the performance of the student in several dimensions — written work,
practical work, oral work, contribution to group exercises, and
personal qualities such as interest and enthusiasm, as well as originality
and flair for the subject.

One teacher does not always deal with all facets of a student's
work. Often a number of individual teachers' assessments have to be
married to produce an overall assessment in the form of, for example,
a lettered grade. At the outset teachers should decide upon the
number of grades or bands of attainment they will use. Five bands or
grades are most frequently used:

A	outstandingly good	10 per cent of students
B	good	20 per cent of students
C	average	40 per cent of students
D	below average	20 per cent of students
E	weak	10 per cent of students

It is important to define attainment in a particular subject and to
identify the separate elements which might be held to constitute
attainment in that subject. The weighting accorded to each element
should indicate its relative importance.

PREPARATION FOR EXTERNAL EXAMINATIONS

Many students will attend courses expecting to pass the appropriate qualifying examinations. There is ample evidence that very good examination results have been obtained by teachers who first create an intense interest in their subject and then secure the active and persistent co-operation of their students. The teacher in Further Education should be able to offer his students something more than the textbook and more than the correspondence course.

A common failing of teachers is the practice of spending an undue proportion of the session on the first lessons of the course: this is understandable because teachers must spend some time in getting to know their students and also their ability to absorb the instruction; but a consequence may be that the later sections of the syllabus may receive scant attention, and to that extent, the examination results may be in jeopardy.

Mock examinations set internally serve to introduce students to the most advantageous methods of answering the written questions set in the external examinations; particularly in the allocation of time, which is available for the number of questions to be answered.

Students should be strongly advised to give thought to the proportion of time available which should be given to each answer, and to avoid spending too much time on some answers to the detriment of the answers to the remaining questions.

All experienced examiners recommend the advisibility of reserving some of the examination period to a revision of the answers; for, in the anxiety and pressure which are ever present with the earnest examinee, omissions of important words or numbers and erratic spelling may be overlooked at the time of actual writing.

It is necessary to impress upon students that examiners have usually a big task before them, for many papers have to be marked and assessed. Their time is valuable and their patience has its limitations. Therefore, advise your students not to waste their time and patience by "padding out" the answers. This trick deceives no one except the perpetrator: for the examiner expects direct answers to his questions and he will either ignore or penalize irrelevances.

INTERNAL EXAMINATIONS

These are set to test from time to time the progress of the students in the classroom, laboratory and workshop. A useful technique is to give students the questions some time in advance of the examination, so that they can collect appropriate information. Ultimately questions can be answered without reference to notes. This technique can reduce tension and produce effective revision.

FURTHER READING

B S Bloom *Taxonomy of Educational Objectives: I. Cognitive Domain*, 1965, Longmans Green

Objective Testing, 1969, City and Guilds of London Institute.

Frank Bacon *Technical Education and Industrial Training.* Issues June–September 1969, 4 articles on Examinations, Testing and Assessment

Douglas Pidgeon and Alfred Yates *An Introduction to Educational Measurement*, 1968, Routledge, Kegan Paul (117 pages)

W Bonney Rust and H F P Harris *Examinations: Pass or Failure*?, Pitman 1967 (112 pages)

14

Teacher Effectiveness

" . . . . a teacher who pays no attention to the effect he is having on the class is like someone who paints with his eyes shut." (M E Foss)

A teacher acquires the art and skills of teaching by (1) knowing the results of his actions upon his students and (2) applying this knowledge to improve his effectiveness. The teacher's knowledge of his effect is related to the effect he is aiming for and the methods he is using. A teacher may be able to recall a dozen principles of learning but show an utter disregard for them in what he does with his classes. Both the new and inexperienced teacher and the veteran can profit from "feedback" on how well he is doing with his classes. First, he may obtain immediate feedback by observing the behaviour of the students before him and questioning them, to test both perception and understanding. Second, he may accept an assessment of his per-performance from a colleague or tutor. Third, he may invite students to complete rating schedules.

SELF-ASSESSMENT

After each lesson or unit of teaching, the teacher may review what has happened and what he has learned by answering such questions as:

Did I do all I set out to do?

If not, why not? Had I too much material or too little?

Did I not allow enough time for students' questions and interruptions?

Did I depend too much upon those students who knew the answers and neglect the slower ones?

Did I manage to keep the class in control? If not was it because I bored them, excited their interest so much that I could not restore order, or was I unable to manage one or two tiresome students?

Would I make any major changes, if I were giving the lesson again?

Shall I have to change my plans for the next lesson as the result of this one?

The teacher should tell himself quite frankly where he thinks he succeeded and where he failed. It is an opportunity for self-appraisement and self-assessment.

LESSON OBSERVATION

It is important for the teacher in training to have unambiguous and constructive criticism from a tutor or supervisor as frequently as possible. Unfortunately most supervisors are too heavily committed to teaching and administration to visit their students often enough. Gradually the practice of viewing telerecordings of students' practice is gaining ground. Quite recently it has been advocated that it would be highly desirable that teachers in further education should make a practice of inviting their colleagues to observe them.

In Chapter 3 a plan was given for a practical lesson in Hairdressing. This lesson was presented in a classroom, monitored by television cameras and viewed by over 100 teachers on four screens in a large college hall. An observation of that lesson is given so as to indicate a number of points on which the supervisor may make an assessment of a lesson and also to raise a number of questions that may lead to discussion of the conduct of a practical lesson.

EXAMPLE OBSERVATION OF A LESSON

Let us remind ourselves of what the teacher may do well or badly in a practical lesson. He will:

1 Tell the students what to do and what to expect.

2 Provide the equipment and watch how they use it.

3 Guide their movements or let them try out an action and then show where they went wrong.

4 Give hints on how to cope with the awkward parts.

5 Encourage students to practise.

6 Let them know whether they have improved or how they stand up to comparison with other students.

Aim: The lesson had a number of objectives:

1 To convey
    (*a*) How the student should stand when operating in the salon.
    (*b*) How he should dress.
    (*c*) How he should set out his tools.
    (*d*) How he should keep them clean and disinfected.
    (*e*) How he should take safety precautions with clothing and tools.
These objectives were clearly stated in the lesson introduction, and are in performance terms what the student would be doing when he was demonstrating mastery of the objectives.

2 To demonstrate the basic set and supervise the practice of:
   (*a*) Combing hair after a shampoo.
   (*b*) Sectioning hair.
   (*c*) Making a pin-curl.
   (*d*) Applying a hair net and ear shields.

Discussion points
1 Should all these objectives be incorporated into a single period of
   instruction lasting . . . .?
2 What performance would be expected from a student at the end
   of this period?

Incentive: The students were encouraged to adopt certain attitudes
to dress, safety and hygiene.

Discussion points
1 Should students be criticized for negative example, e.g. Mr P for
   wearing his sleeves to the wrist, Miss S for wearing an unbuttoned
   overall, having clips in her breast pocket and chewing gum?
2 Should the teacher give negative instruction by asking students to
   spot his deliberate mistakes, e.g. holding clips in the mouth while
   pinning up curls, placing the comb in the breast pocket at the
   time of putting rollers in the hair?

Demonstration
Each demonstration: (*a*) combing hair, (*b*) sectioning hair, (*c*) making
a pin-curl, (*d*) applying a hair net and ear shields, was first shown at
normal speed, then at a slower speed, and finally at normal speed.
Oral guidance was necessary to focus students' attention and to
justify the mode of operation, e.g. "Commence at the end of the hair,
combing hair from the ends up, to avoid discomfort to clients".

Two students stood on either side of the client. It is doubtful
whether, even though the student group was so small, they would
always be in a position to see what the teacher was doing. This could
be obviated by introducing swivel chairs, at least for the teaching
demonstration, into college salons.

Discussion points: Can students grasp more from slowed-down
demonstrations? Would the 8 mm loop or slowed-down photography
serve the purpose better?

Hints: It is the hairdressing teacher's responsibility to evolve a set of
hints which he presents at appropriate points in his demonstration if
he wishes his students to understand what he is doing and to respond
appropriately in their own practice. Emphasis was given to important
movements by the use of verbal arrowheads, e.g. "Hold roller at 45
degrees away from the hair" and "Roll hair over, using thumbs as
two needles".

Perceptual cues: The teacher's greatest difficulty is in conveying to his students how the information or feedback, received by sight and touch and sound on how well he is performing, makes him automatically modify his movements, stance, thumb pressure. In the putting in of a pin-curl one of ten or so current methods was shown.

Discussion points
1 Should pinning up start at the front or at the back?
2 Does the use of a simple method make students too inflexible?
3 Are different methods necessary at different parts of the head?

Visual Aids: The object of intermediary visuals such as those shown should be to give visual guidance at appropriate points in the demonstrations. They should magnify the whole task and allow the student to see clearly what is to be done, and help him modify his responses.

Discussion Point
Should the visuals precede the oral commentary?

Knowledge of Results

Unless a practice lesson on CCTV requires an inordinately long span of attention from the viewer, it is scarcely possible to present continuously in a live demonstration, the practice of the students and terminal knowledge of their results. This means that one of the most important aspects of the teaching-learning continuum is omitted.

Instruction on CCTV

The experiment demonstrated two things: first that a certain procedure is feasible and second that it can be precisely analysed as a system of variables.

The teacher decides *what* the cameras are to transmit but a producer should suggest *how*. The producer's continuing concern should be to help the teacher think first of what will be *seen* not *said*. He will guide the teacher in matters of visuals:

1 Use of contrasts of light and dark
2 Display of three-dimensional models
3 Pull-cards
4 Use of students and how they help fulfil the purpose of the lesson.

This experiment produced an information fall-out which raised questions about:

1 What constitutes a well-structured opening and close?
2 How much "fill-material"?
3 What kind of teacher-pacing is needed to reach the viewer and create dramatic impact?

The author is indebted to Simon Beresford (Lecturer in Hairdressing at Liverpool College of Crafts and Catering) for collaboration in this experiment.

STUDENTS' VIEWS

"It is much easier to fool one's colleagues than one's students."[1]
Students who have spent, say 36 to 108 hours, or one hour per week to three hours per week, during a normal session of 36 weeks, are in a position to give a reliable view of a teacher's effectiveness. In 1968 the *Report of the Board for Prices and Incomes on the Pay of University Teachers in Great Britain* stated: "We do not pretend that the assessment of the quality of an individual's teaching will be easy, but there are a number of guidelines . . . . one of these is assessment by students, not through a popularity poll, but through a carefully drafted questionnaire". The evaluation of teachers in relation to their students may be of several kinds: (i) of the personal satisfaction of the teacher, (ii) of the desirable changes they produce in students and (iii) of the aspects of teachers which are considered to have a relationship with desirable changes in students.

There is wide variation in definitions of "the good teacher", and measurement of effectiveness needs to take into account the teacher, the student and the subject. A considerable amount of investigation has been carried out in America to determine the essential factors in good teaching. Rating scales have been derived out of the work of numerous investigators as suitable for the rating of teachers by students.

In wide use is the Purdue Rating Scale which contains ten aspects which students are asked to rate:

1 Interest in subject
2 Sympathetic attitude towards students
3 Fairness in grading
4 Liberal and progressive attitude
5 Presentation of subject matter
6 Sense of proportion and humour
7 Self-reliance and confidence
8 Personal peculiarities
9 Personal appearance
10 Stimulating intellectual curiosity

[1] L Cole *The Background to College Teaching* (p 350), New York, Farrar and Rinehart, 1940.

This is a graphic scale. The students are asked to make a mark on each line at the point which most nearly describes the teacher with reference to the aspect being considered:

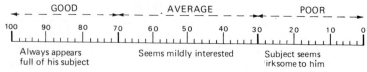

Fig 14.1 *Interest in subject*

It will be seen that there are three areas for each aspect— "Good", "Average", "Poor". Each aspect should be assessed separately without reference to the other qualities. If a teacher wishes to find out what effect he is having upon his students he should distribute the scales and ask the students to pass judgement. It has been objected that students would treat the assessment scales as a joke, would be afraid to express their true estimate, would take the opportunity to express their dislike, and would not be capable of recognizing good teaching. What may emerge from the students' ratings is a profile of the teacher which he should consider with a view to improvement of "qualities" which are consistently graded low. It is better that students' opinions of teachers should be brought out into the open and used positively.

EVALUATION OF COURSES

At the end of any course of instruction the teacher should ask himself: "How much have the students learned?" and "Were the objectives of the course realized?" and "Did the programme fulfil the needs of the students?" For a course entitled "Decimal Currency and You" the course objectives were given as follows:

At the end of the course student will:

1 Know the names and values of decimal coins.
2 Be able to shop and give change in decimal and £ s. d. shops.
3 Be able to convert £ s. d. to £ p.
4 Be able to write decimal amounts on cheques, invoices, bills.

An objective-type test was constructed to assess the performance and achievement of the students. As the students, twenty-five in number, were all adults, it was thought that there would probably be some resistance to attempting to answer a questionnaire. Teaching involves change and few people willingly accept change. Since testing attempts to measure the degree of change, it implies a direct or indirect judgement of everyone who is being assessed. Accordingly the rubric did not ask students to write their name on the quiz sheet but provided them with a method of marking their own answers and obtaining knowledge of results.

CURRENCY QUIZ

The following questions are meant to give you and us an idea if you have learnt anything from this course. Please put your answers in the *answer* column.

When everyone appears to have finished the quiz (approx 15 minutes), the answers will be read out, and you are asked to enter a Tick or Cross against the appropriate answers.

Please do *not* put your name on the quiz.

Please hand in at the end of the discussion on this quiz.

		Answer	*Tick/ Cross*
1	In decimal currency, how many different coins *will* there be?		
2	What is the value of 6d. in decimal currency?		
3	What is the value of 2s. 6d. in decimal currency?		
4	Give an alternative way of writing 48p.		
5	Which of the following are incorrectly written: a) £2.06 b) 3.50 c) 2p d) 3.21p?		
6	Using the £ sign write down: (*a*) Eight new pence. (*b*) One pound and one half new penny. (*c*) Eighty pence. (*d*) Two and a half new pence. (*e*) Thirty-two and a half pence.		
7	How would the sum of eleven pounds thirty-three pence appear in the figures space on a cheque?	£	
8	Show the *two* acceptable ways of writing the following: (*a*) Five and a half new pence. (*b*) Twenty-one pence.	. . . . . or . . . . or	
9	Write down the following amounts in words: (*a*) 7½p. (*b*) £65.10. (*c*) £42.85.		
10	If 9 gallons of petrol cost £3.06, what is the cost per gallon?		
11	Give the cost of: 12 articles at £2.32½ each. 5 articles at 89p each.		

12 Convert the following into decimal currency:
    (*a*) £4 13s. 6d.
    (*b*) £10 11s 6d.
    (*c*) £2 15s 0d.

13 Find 5 per cent of £4.60.

14 Find 10 per cent of £3.45.

15 Subtract £97.50 from £162.50.

16 Articles cost 24p. A customer gives 2 × 10p
    and one shilling. What change does he receive?

17 Articles cost £1.39. A customer gives in 30
    shillings. What change does he receive?

18 Convert the following invoice to decimal currency.

	£	s.	d.
6 chromium showers at £4 7s. 6d.	26	5	0
Less 10% discount.	2	12	6
	£23	12	6

19 Rewrite the following restaurant bill in decimal
    currency.

	£	s.	d.
2 Oxtail soups at 3/-		6	0
2 Portions roast beef at 8/6		17	0
2 vegetables at 3/6		7	0
1 Ginger sponge at 2/3		2	3
1 Apple tart at 2/9		2	9
2 coffees at 1/6		3	0
	£1	18	0
10% service charge.		3	10
	£2	1	10

20 When is "D Day"?

An analysis of the students' replies provided useful evidence of
whether there was the correct quality or quantity of suitably
comprehensive instruction at each point of the course.

In addition an evaluation questionnaire was prepared to tap the
participant's views on:

1 Reasons for attending the course.

2 Problems experienced.

3 Success rating.

4 Proposals for changes in future courses.

QUESTIONNAIRE ON THE COURSE
REDECIMALIZATION OF CURRENCY

Purpose

You have just completed a short course on the Decimalization of British Currency and in order that we, who have been arranging the course, may collect information which will help us to improve subsequent courses of this type, you are now asked to complete the following questionnaire about the course. Where a choice of answers is offered please tick the one which you feel to be most correct.

1 (Motivation) Did you attend the course to obtain information which may be of value:
    (*a*) In your employment?
    (*b*) For shopping and household finances?
    (*c*) Out of general interest?

2 (Standard) Did you find that in general the instruction given seemed to be:
    (*a*) Too hard?
    (*b*) Too easy?
    (*c*) Just right?

3 Which part of the course did you find easiest to follow? (e.g. coin recognition, use of decimals, conversion, etc.)

. . . .

4 Which part of the course did you find hardest to follow?

. . . .

5 (Duration) Did you find the length of the course and sessions –
                                                Course   *Sessions*
    (*a*) Too long.
    (*b*) Too short.
    (*c*) Just right.
        (If (*a*) or (*b*), by how much?   . . . .)

6 (Deficiencies) Are there any major items in the course about which you still feel unsure? (Specify.). . . . .
. . . .

7 Do you feel that any useful points which should have been dealt with were omitted from the course?   . . . .
. . . .

8 (Reinforcement) Was there:
   (*a*) Too much repetition?
   (*b*) Insufficient care in pointing out each occasion when an
         important point or principle was being used?
   (*c*) A reasonable opportunity to use over and over the principles
         which are really important?

9 To what degree have you enjoyed the course:
   (*a*) Little or not at all?
   (*b*) Moderately?
   (*c*) Very much?

10 Please add any comments or suggestions overleaf which you feel
might help future students of your course.
                Thank you for your help and co-operation

CONCLUSION

All teaching techniques are a function of an activity, social and
dynamic in nature. Teaching centres are becoming larger and larger
units and their range of activities wider and wider. The reactions of
students play a greater part in developing teaching methods. The
teacher and student are increasingly considered to be a part of a
learning system. This system places teachers who enjoy their work
and have close and friendly relations with their students in a
strategic position to do more for them than most other people.

FURTHER READING

H L Hill "Lesson Observation," *The Technical Journal*, February 1967 (pages
7–9)

Bob Oxtoby "Lectures and Lecturers," *The Technical Journal*, June 1969
(pages 19–20)

David Kimber "Evaluation of Training," *Industrial Training International*,
June 1970 (pages 276–278)

Index

Abilities, 112
Academic development, 17
Aids, 94
Algorithm, 63
Assessment, continuous, 120
    scales, 128 self, 123
Assignments, 111
Assimilation, 37, 47
Attention, 36, 55

Bloom, B S, 33
Breadth, 100
Burgess, Norman, 89

Case-study, 88
CCTV, 126
Chalkboard, 64, 72-3, 95-7
Class management, 105
Communication, non-verbal, 58
Contact hours, 12
Controlling bodies, 4
Course design, 41
Courses, non-vocational, 2
    vocational, 2
Crowder, Dr N, 31
Cues, perceptual, 126
Curiosity, 34

Demonstration, 51, 53, 75, 77-81, 125
Dictation, 64
Discipline, 106, 108
Discovery, 34
Duane, Michael, 107